SQL 101 Crash Course

Comprehensive Guide to SQL Fundamentals and Practical Applications

Emrys Callahan

Copyright © 2023 by GitforGits

Published by: GitforGits
Publisher: Sonal Dhandre
www.gitforgits.com
support@gitforgits.com

Printed in India

First Printing: May 2023

ISBN: 978-8119177141

Cover Design by: Kitten Publishing

For permission to use material from this book, please contact GitforGits at support@gitforgits.com.

Content

Preface

SQL 101 Crash Course is a comprehensive beginner's guide that takes you through the world of SQL, right from understanding databases to mastering complex queries. This book is designed to provide you with a solid foundation in SQL, along with practical examples and real-world scenarios to reinforce your learning.

In this book, you'll explore the key concepts of databases and their structure while getting started with SQLite Studio, a versatile SQL tool. You'll dive deep into the fundamentals of SQL queries, turning raw data into meaningful information, and working with tables, multiple tables, and their relationships. You'll also learn how to harness the power of SQL functions and subqueries to optimize your queries and retrieve data more efficiently. As you progress, you'll delve into the world of views, joins, and advanced SQL topics such as transactions, stored procedures, and performance tuning. The book concludes with two sample databases, where you'll put your newfound knowledge to the test and gain hands-on experience.

This book promises a smooth learning journey for aspiring SQL developers, enabling them to build robust and efficient databases. The book's step-by-step approach ensures that even complete beginners can grasp complex concepts with ease. By the end of this book, you'll emerge as a smart SQL developer, equipped with the skills and knowledge to tackle real-world database challenges.

In this book you will learn how to:

- Master SQL fundamentals and best practices.
- Learn to create, modify, and optimize tables.
- Understand and implement table relationships.
- Execute complex queries with ease and confidence.
- Leverage SQL functions for powerful data manipulation.
- Utilize subqueries and derived tables effectively.
- Create and manage views for enhanced data access.
- Apply advanced SQL techniques for optimized performance.
- Hands-on experience with real-world sample databases.
- Begin your journey as a skilled SQL developer

GitforGits

Prerequisites

This book requires no prior knowledge to get started, making it an ideal read for those looking to pursue careers in database administration, business analytics, or business intelligence. Its accessibility ensures that an unwavering passion for learning SQL is all you need to effortlessly progress through the book's content.

Codes Usage

Are you in need of some helpful code examples to assist you in your programming and documentation? Look no further! Our book offers a wealth of supplemental material, including code examples and exercises.

Not only is this book here to aid you in getting your job done, but you have our permission to use the example code in your programs and documentation. However, please note that if you are reproducing a significant portion of the code, we do require you to contact us for permission.

But don't worry, using several chunks of code from this book in your program or answering a question by citing our book and quoting example code does not require permission. But if you do choose to give credit, an attribution typically includes the title, author, publisher, and ISBN. For example, "SQL 101 Crash Course by Emrys Callahan".

If you are unsure whether your intended use of the code examples falls under fair use or the permissions outlined above, please do not hesitate to reach out to us at support@gitforgits.com.

We are happy to assist and clarify any concerns.

Acknowledgement

I owe a tremendous debt of gratitude to GitforGits, for their unflagging enthusiasm and wise counsel throughout the entire process of writing this book. Their knowledge and careful editing helped make sure the piece was useful for people of all reading levels and comprehension skills. In addition, I'd like to thank everyone involved in the publishing process for their efforts in making this book a reality. Their efforts, from copyediting to advertising, made the project what it is today.

Finally, I'd like to express my gratitude to everyone who has shown me unconditional love and encouragement throughout my life. Their support was crucial to the completion of this book. I appreciate your help with this endeavour and your continued interest in my career.

Prologue

Welcome to the "SQL 101 Crash Course," an in-depth instructional resource designed to help you learn SQL from start and gain the necessary skills to become an expert SQL developer. Structured Query Language, more often known as SQL, is the language of choice for interacting with relational database systems. SQL is now a necessary skill for professionals working in a variety of fields, including software development, data analysis, and business intelligence. This is because of the ever-increasing significance of data in our modern society.

The goal of this book is to provide you a strong foundation in SQL, beginning with the fundamental ideas of databases and their structures and progressing all the way up to the intricate details of more sophisticated SQL approaches. First, we'll go over a brief introduction to relational database management systems (RDBMS), followed by a discussion of the duties of a SQL developer. After that, you will delve into the more practical parts of SQL, and you will learn how to build up your environment by making use of SQLite Studio, which is a flexible SQL tool.

As you move through the chapters, you will investigate the principles of SQL queries, discover how to transform data into information with meaning, and practice working with tables, multiple databases, and the relationships between them. You will also learn how to optimize your queries and get data in a more effective manner by utilizing SQL functions and subqueries, which you will learn about.

In the later chapters of the book, we will go over more sophisticated topics such as views, joins, transactions, stored procedures, and approaches for performance tuning. The book comes to a close with two sample databases, in which you will practice applying what you've learned in the book to real-life settings. This book is written in a way that makes it accessible to a wide variety of readers, including those who have never worked with SQL before and those who have some familiarity with the language but are looking to improve their abilities. The systematic method combined with real-world examples makes even the most difficult ideas simple to understand and implement. As you progress through the chapters, you will develop the self-assurance and skill necessary to take on the issues that are encountered in the real world with databases.

You will start on an exciting adventure into the world of SQL with the help of the "SQL 101 Crash Course," gaining skills that are useful and in high demand across a variety of sectors along the way. In your efforts to become an expert SQL programmer, we hope that you will find this book to be an invaluable resource.

Chapter 1: Introduction to Databases and SQL

Necessity of a Database

In today's digital age, data is the lifeblood of businesses, governments, and organizations worldwide. Data is used to drive decision-making, understand customer needs, optimize processes, and uncover valuable insights that lead to growth and innovation. To manage, organize, and analyze this data effectively, we need databases.

A database is an organized collection of structured data that allows efficient storage, retrieval, and manipulation of information. Without databases, data would be scattered across disparate systems, making it difficult to access, analyze, or use effectively. Databases provide a centralized and structured system for storing, organizing, and managing data, making it easier to extract insights and draw meaningful conclusions.

What is a Database?

A database is a sophisticated system that stores, organizes, and manages data in a structured format, enabling users to access and manipulate the information with ease. By providing efficient ways to store, retrieve, and manipulate data, databases ensure data consistency, security, and integrity. They play a critical role in various applications, from simple record-keeping systems to complex data management solutions. Databases can be broadly categorized into two primary types: relational and non-relational databases.

Relational databases, also known as SQL databases, store data in a tabular format, with rows and columns resembling a spreadsheet. Each row in a table represents a unique data record, while each column signifies a specific data attribute. These databases use a structured query language (SQL), which is a standardized programming language to interact with and manipulate the stored data. Relational databases are designed for managing structured data and are often used in applications that require complex queries, transactions, and data consistency.

Non-relational databases, commonly referred to as NoSQL databases, store data in various formats, such as key-value, document, column-family, or graph. Unlike relational databases, they do not rely on a fixed schema and can accommodate unstructured or semi-structured data. Non-relational databases are designed with flexibility, scalability, and high performance in mind, making them suitable for handling vast volumes of data or applications that demand rapid data access. They are often employed in big data, real-time analytics, and distributed computing scenarios where traditional relational databases might struggle to scale or maintain performance.

The Rise of Databases

The rise of databases can be traced back to the 1960s when the first database management systems (DBMS) were developed. The need for efficient data storage and retrieval systems grew with the increasing use of computers in various industries. In 1970, Dr. Edgar F. Codd, a computer scientist at IBM, proposed the relational database model, which revolutionized the way databases were designed and used. This model led to the development of the first commercial relational database management systems (RDBMS) in the late 1970s and early 1980s, such as Oracle and IBM's DB2.

The demand for databases continued to grow with the advent of the internet, as businesses needed to store and manage vast amounts of data generated by online transactions, social media, and other digital platforms. The rise of big data and the need to process and analyze massive data sets led to the development of NoSQL databases, which provided greater flexibility and scalability than traditional relational databases.

Today, databases play a crucial role in virtually every industry, from finance and healthcare to e-commerce and social media. As the volume, variety, and velocity of data continue to grow, databases will remain an essential tool for managing and extracting value from this data.

Database Terminologies

Understanding the terminology used in databases is essential for grasping the underlying concepts and working with databases effectively. In this section, we will explore common terms and their meanings to enhance your knowledge and efficiency while working with databases. Familiarizing yourself with these terms, such as tables, rows, columns, primary keys, foreign keys, relationships, normalization, and SQL, will help you better comprehend database structures, design, and manipulation. Gaining this understanding will ultimately enable you to optimize database performance and maintain data integrity.

Data

Information stored in a database, which can be in various forms, such as text, numbers, dates, or multimedia content like images or videos.

Table

A table is a collection of related data organized in rows and columns. Each row represents a record, and each column represents a field or attribute of the record.

Schema

A schema is the structure and organization of a database, including tables, fields, relationships, and constraints. It defines how data is stored and organized within the database.

Record (or Row)

A record, also known as a row, is a single set of related data in a table. It contains data for each attribute or field defined in the table schema.

Field (or Column)

A field, also known as a column, is a specific attribute or data element within a table. Each field has a defined data type, such as integer, text, or date, which determines the kind of data it can store.

Primary Key

A primary key is a unique identifier for each record in a table. It ensures that each record can be uniquely identified and accessed. A primary key can be a single field or a combination of fields.

Foreign Key

A foreign key is a field or a set of fields in one table that refers to the primary key of another table. It is used to establish relationships between tables and ensure data integrity.

Index

An index is a database object that helps speed up data retrieval. It is created on one or more fields in a table, allowing the database to find records more quickly when searching for specific values.

Query

A query is a request for data from the database. In relational databases, queries are written using SQL, which allows users to retrieve, insert, update, or delete data from the database.

Relationship

A relationship is a connection between two or more tables in a database. Relationships help to establish links between related data and ensure data integrity.

Elements of a Database

Data Types

Data types define the kind of data that can be stored in a field. Common data types include integer, float, text, date, and boolean. Each database system may have its specific data types, such as VARCHAR, DECIMAL, or TIMESTAMP.

Constraints

Constraints are rules applied to fields or tables to maintain data integrity and consistency. Examples of constraints include primary key, foreign key, unique, not null, and check constraints.

Views

A view is a virtual table that displays the result of a query. Views can be used to simplify complex queries, provide a specific view of the data for different users, or enhance data security by limiting access to sensitive information.

Triggers

A trigger is a database object that automatically executes a specific action, such as inserting, updating, or deleting data, when a specified event occurs. Triggers can be used to maintain data consistency, enforce business rules, or audit changes in the database.

Stored Procedures

A stored procedure is a precompiled set of SQL statements that can be executed as a single command. Stored procedures can help improve database performance, reduce network traffic, and enforce data integrity.

Transactions

A transaction is a sequence of one or more database operations, such as inserting, updating, or deleting data, that are executed as a single unit of work. Transactions ensure that the database remains in a consistent state even if some operations fail, by adhering to the ACID properties: Atomicity, Consistency, Isolation, and Durability.

Normalization

Normalization is the process of organizing data in a database to minimize redundancy and improve data integrity. It involves decomposing tables into smaller, related tables and defining relationships between them. Normalization follows various normal forms, such as First

Normal Form (1NF), Second Normal Form (2NF), and Third Normal Form (3NF).

Denormalization

Denormalization is the process of intentionally adding redundancy to a database to improve performance. By duplicating data or combining tables, denormalization can reduce the need for complex joins and speed up query execution. However, it may also increase the risk of data inconsistency and require more storage space.

Backup and Recovery

Backup is the process of creating a copy of the database to protect against data loss or corruption. Recovery refers to the process of restoring a database from a backup to recover lost or damaged data. Database systems typically provide tools and mechanisms for managing backups and recovery.

Database Security

Database security involves protecting the data, the database system, and the users from unauthorized access, data breaches, or other security threats. Common database security measures include user authentication and authorization, data encryption, and network security.

By understanding these terminologies and elements, you will be better equipped to work with databases and apply the knowledge to real-world scenarios. As you delve deeper into SQL and database management, these concepts will serve as the foundation for more advanced techniques and topics.

Introduction to RDBMS

What is RDBMS?

A Relational Database Management System (RDBMS) is a type of database management system that stores and manages data in a structured format, using tables with rows and columns. RDBMS is based on the relational model, which was introduced by Dr. Edgar F. Codd in 1970. The relational model organizes data into tables, also known as relations, and allows users to define relationships between these tables. RDBMSs provide various features to ensure data consistency, integrity, security, and performance.

Some popular RDBMSs include MySQL, PostgreSQL, Oracle Database, Microsoft SQL Server, and SQLite.

<u>Why SQL essential for RDBMS?</u>

SQL, or Structured Query Language, is the standard language used to communicate with and manipulate data in a relational database. SQL is essential for working with RDBMS because it provides a consistent and efficient way to interact with the data stored in relational databases.

Some of the reasons why SQL is crucial for RDBMS include:

Standardized Language: SQL is an ANSI (American National Standards Institute) and ISO (International Organization for Standardization) standard, ensuring that the same SQL syntax and commands can be used across different RDBMSs with minimal variations.

Powerful Data Manipulation: SQL allows users to perform various operations on the data, such as inserting, updating, deleting, and retrieving data. It also supports complex queries, aggregations, and data transformation, enabling users to derive meaningful insights from the stored data.

Data Definition and Management: SQL enables users to define the structure of the database, create tables, set data types, and specify constraints, such as primary keys and foreign keys. It also provides commands to manage database objects, such as creating, altering, or dropping tables, indexes, and views.

Transactions and Concurrency Control: SQL supports transactions, which ensure that the database remains consistent even if some operations fail. It also provides mechanisms for managing concurrent access to the database, preventing conflicts and ensuring data integrity.

Security and Access Control: SQL provides features for managing user authentication and authorization, enabling database administrators to control access to the data and restrict specific operations, such as inserting, updating, or deleting records.

Compatibility and Interoperability: Since SQL is a standardized language, it enables developers and database administrators to work with various RDBMSs without having to learn a new language for each system. This promotes compatibility and interoperability between different database platforms and applications.

Key SQL Concepts and Definitions

To work effectively with SQL, it's essential to understand some key concepts and definitions. The SELECT statement, WHERE clause, JOINs, GROUP BY clause, HAVING clause, ORDER BY clause, Functions, Subqueries, and Indexes are fundamental concepts in SQL, essential for querying and managing data in relational databases. Understanding these concepts helps in creating efficient and maintainable SQL queries.

The given below are some fundamental aspects of SQL that one must learn:

SQL Statements

SQL statements are the building blocks of SQL commands used to interact with the database.

They can be divided into several categories:
- Data Definition Language (DDL): DDL statements are used to define and manage database objects like tables, indexes, and views. Common DDL statements include CREATE, ALTER, and DROP.
- Data Manipulation Language (DML): DML statements allow you to insert, update, delete, and retrieve data in the database. Common DML statements include SELECT, INSERT, UPDATE, and DELETE.
- Data Control Language (DCL): DCL statements are used to manage user permissions and access control. Common DCL statements include GRANT and REVOKE.
- Transaction Control Language (TCL): TCL statements help manage transactions and ensure data consistency. Common TCL statements include COMMIT, ROLLBACK, and SAVEPOINT.

SELECT Statement

The SELECT statement is a cornerstone of SQL, allowing users to retrieve data from one or more tables. The statement supports specifying the columns to be retrieved, filtering data with conditions, joining tables based on related columns, grouping data, and ordering the results. Mastering the SELECT statement enables users to extract relevant and meaningful information from vast amounts of data stored in databases.

WHERE Clause

The WHERE clause works in tandem with SELECT, UPDATE, and DELETE statements to filter data based on specific conditions. It employs comparison operators, logical operators, and functions to define these conditions, ensuring that only the desired data is retrieved, updated, or deleted. The WHERE clause is crucial for narrowing down datasets and obtaining precise results.

JOINs

JOINs combine data from two or more tables based on related columns, enabling users to retrieve information from multiple tables in a single query. Several types of JOINs exist, including INNER JOIN, OUTER JOIN (LEFT, RIGHT, and FULL), and CROSS JOIN. Understanding the differences between these JOIN types and when to use them is vital for efficient and accurate data retrieval.

GROUP BY Clause

The GROUP BY clause works with aggregate functions like COUNT, SUM, AVG, MIN, and MAX to group data based on one or more columns and perform calculations on each group. This functionality is particularly useful for summarizing and aggregating large datasets, providing insights into trends and patterns within the data.

HAVING Clause

The HAVING clause, used in conjunction with the GROUP BY clause, filters grouped data based on a condition involving an aggregate function. The HAVING clause refines the results of the GROUP BY clause, ensuring that only the relevant groups are returned in the query.

ORDER BY Clause

The ORDER BY clause sorts the results of a SELECT statement based on one or more columns, either in ascending (ASC) or descending (DESC) order. Properly ordered data facilitates easier analysis and interpretation by users.

Functions

SQL provides various built-in functions to perform calculations, manipulate strings, work with dates and times, and more. Functions fall into categories like aggregate functions, scalar functions, and window functions, each serving specific purposes within queries. Mastering SQL functions empowers users to manipulate and transform data in a myriad of ways, tailoring the output to their needs.

Subqueries

Subqueries, or queries embedded within another query, allow users to leverage the result of an inner query in an outer query. Subqueries can be used in SELECT, FROM, WHERE, and HAVING clauses, providing flexibility and enabling complex query structures for advanced data retrieval.

Indexes

Indexes, as database objects, enhance data retrieval performance. Created on one or more columns in a table, indexes enable databases to find records more quickly when searching for specific values. Properly designed and implemented indexes can greatly improve query performance, ensuring that applications run smoothly and efficiently.

Understanding these key concepts and definitions in SQL will provide you with a solid foundation for working with relational databases. Not just that, mastering these fundamental SQL concepts primarily, SELECT statement, WHERE clause, JOINs, GROUP BY clause, HAVING clause, ORDER BY clause, Functions, Subqueries, and Indexes empowers users to create efficient and effective queries, unlocking the full potential of relational databases. As you gain experience and confidence, you can explore more advanced SQL techniques and features to optimize your queries and manage complex database systems.

Summary

This chapter provides an overview of databases, SQL, and the journey of a SQL Developer. It begins by explaining the necessity of databases and their evolution over time. Databases help store, organize, and manage data efficiently, enabling businesses to derive insights, make informed decisions, and streamline their processes.

We then delve into key terminologies and elements of a database, such as tables, records, fields, primary keys, foreign keys, and schemas. These concepts serve as the foundation for understanding database management and working with SQL. We also discuss the concept of a relational database management system (RDBMS), which is based on the relational model introduced by Dr. Edgar F. Codd. To master SQL, it's crucial to understand key concepts and definitions, such as SQL statements (DDL, DML, DCL, and TCL), SELECT statement, WHERE clause, JOINs, GROUP BY and HAVING clauses, ORDER BY clause, functions, subqueries, and indexes. These concepts provide a solid foundation for working with relational databases and exploring more advanced SQL techniques. The journey of a SQL Developer involves various tasks, such as designing and implementing database structures, writing and optimizing queries, developing and maintaining stored procedures and functions, integrating and transforming data, ensuring data quality and integrity, performance tuning and optimization, managing database security and access control, implementing backup and recovery strategies, collaborating with cross-functional teams, and continuously learning and growing professionally.

By understanding the importance of databases, SQL, and the role of a SQL Developer, readers can appreciate the value of learning SQL and mastering the concepts covered in this book. As you progress through the chapters, you'll gain the knowledge and skills needed to succeed in a rewarding career as a SQL Developer.

Chapter 2: Setting Up Your SQL Environment

In this chapter, we delve into the significance of utilizing an SQL tool for effective database management and introduce SQLite Studio, a robust and user-friendly solution. SQL tools are essential in simplifying the process of working with databases, enabling users to create, modify, and maintain data structures more efficiently. SQLite Studio is a powerful tool that boasts a range of features, including a visually appealing interface, advanced query capabilities, and data manipulation options. Through this comprehensive tool, users can streamline their database management experience, improve productivity, and gain better insights into their data, ultimately leading to more informed decision-making.

The Importance of a SQL Tool

Working with databases demands a user-friendly and efficient method to interact with the data and manage database objects effectively. A SQL tool serves as a comprehensive interface for executing SQL queries, managing database objects, visualizing table structures, and performing various other tasks. By streamlining the process of interacting with databases, SQL tools make it more efficient and less susceptible to errors. SQL tools come equipped with a range of features that enhance productivity and code quality. Syntax highlighting is one such feature that adds color coding to SQL code, making it easier to read and understand. This visual aid helps developers quickly identify and rectify errors, thus reducing debugging time.

Autocompletion is another valuable feature provided by SQL tools. It offers suggestions while typing queries, saving time and effort by reducing the need to remember or look up complex database object names, keywords, or functions. This feature not only expedites the coding process but also minimizes the chances of typos or syntax errors. Error reporting is a critical aspect of SQL tools, as it promptly highlights any errors in the code, providing developers with clear and actionable feedback. This real-time feedback allows for swift identification and correction of mistakes, preventing potential issues from escalating.

Introducing SQLite Studio

SQLite Studio is an open-source, cross-platform SQL tool that has been specifically developed for managing SQLite databases. It boasts a user-friendly interface, which makes it an ideal choice for beginners who are eager to learn and work with SQL queries and database management. With its lightweight design and no installation requirements, SQLite Studio can be quickly and easily launched, making it perfect for performing swift database management tasks or for learning SQL in a hassle-free manner.

The software supports various operating systems, including Windows, macOS, and Linux, ensuring accessibility to a broad range of users. Some of its notable features include syntax highlighting, autocompletion, and error checking, which greatly enhance the user experience and facilitate efficient coding. SQLite Studio also allows users to easily manage tables, indexes, triggers, and views, while providing import and export functionality for various formats such as CSV, JSON, and XML.

SQLite Studio Features

SQLite Studio offers numerous features that make managing databases and writing SQL queries easier and more efficient. Some of its key features include:

User-friendly Interface: SQLite Studio's intuitive interface makes it easy to navigate and manage your databases. The main window consists of a tree view of your database objects, an SQL editor for writing queries, and a results pane for displaying query results.

Syntax Highlighting and Autocompletion: SQLite Studio provides syntax highlighting and autocompletion for SQL keywords, table names, and column names, making it easier to write and read SQL queries.

Database Object Management: SQLite Studio allows you to create, modify, and delete tables, indexes, views, and triggers directly from its interface. You can also visualize table structures and relationships using its built-in diagramming tool.

Import and Export Data: With SQLite Studio, you can easily import data from CSV, JSON, or XML files and export data to various formats, such as CSV, JSON, XML, and HTML.

Query History and Favorites: SQLite Studio keeps track of your executed queries, allowing you to revisit previous queries or save them as favorites for quick access.

Error Reporting and Query Formatting: SQLite Studio provides error reporting and suggestions to help you fix issues in your SQL queries. It also offers a query formatter to make your SQL code more readable and consistent.

Customizable Interface: SQLite Studio allows you to customize its appearance and behavior according to your preferences. You can change the color scheme, font size, and other visual settings, as well as configure keyboard shortcuts and plugins.

Cross-platform Compatibility: SQLite Studio is compatible with Windows, macOS, and Linux, enabling you to work with SQLite databases on your preferred operating system.

By using SQLite Studio, you can harness the full potential of SQLite databases and write efficient SQL queries with ease. As you progress through this book, SQLite Studio will serve as a valuable tool for practicing the concepts and techniques covered in each chapter.

Installing and Setting Up SQLite Studio

In this section, we'll walkthrough through the process of installing and setting up SQLite Studio on a Windows computer, step by step.

Download SQLite Studio

Visit the SQLite Studio download page at:
https://github.com/pawelsalawa/sqlitestudio/releases

Under the "Downloads" section, locate the latest version of SQLite Studio for Windows and download any of the package type like Installer or Portable. I would recommend to select the file named as 'sqlitestudio_x64-3.4.4.zip'

Click on the download link for the Windows version, and the download will begin.

Extract the SQLite Studio ZIP File

Once the download is complete, locate the downloaded ZIP file in your "Downloads" folder or the folder where you saved the file.

Right-click the ZIP file and select "Extract All..." from the context menu.

Choose the destination folder where you want to extract SQLite Studio. You can keep the default folder or select a different one by clicking the "Browse..." button.

Click "Extract" to extract the contents of the ZIP file to the chosen folder.

Launch SQLite Studio

Navigate to the folder where you extracted SQLite Studio.

Locate the "SQLiteStudio.exe" file (it should have an icon with the SQLite Studio logo).

Double-click the "SQLiteStudio.exe" file to launch SQLite Studio.

Configure SQLite Studio

After launching SQLite Studio, you may want to configure its settings according to your preferences. To do this:

Click on the "Configuration" menu at the top of the SQLite Studio window.

Select "General Configuration" from the dropdown menu.

In the "Configuration" window, you can customize various settings, such as appearance, shortcuts, data editors, and more. Modify these settings as desired.

Click "Apply" to save your changes, and then click "OK" to close the "Configuration" window.

Create or Open a Database

To create a new SQLite database:

Click on the "Database" menu at the top of the SQLite Studio window.

Select "Add a database" from the dropdown menu.

Choose a name for your new database and select a location to save it.

Click "Save" to create the new database.

To open an existing SQLite database:

Click on the "Database" menu at the top of the SQLite Studio window.

Select "Add a database" from the dropdown menu.

In the file picker dialog, navigate to the location of the SQLite database file you want to open (it should have a ".sqlite", ".db", or ".sqlite3" extension).

Click "Open" to add the database to SQLite Studio.

You can now celebrate, as the installation and configuration of SQLite Studio on your Windows machine has been completed without any problems. You can practice the SQL concepts discussed in this book by using it to create, maintain, and query SQLite databases. Additionally, you can use it to practice SQL.

Understanding Structure of a Database

Before we begin creating our first database, it's crucial to understand the fundamental components of a database and their relationships. A database is a collection of organized data that allows for efficient storage, retrieval, and manipulation. In a relational database management system (RDBMS) like SQLite, data is stored in tables that are related to one another.

The structure of a database can be broken down into the following components:

Database: A database is a container for all the related data, tables, and other objects. It serves as the primary unit for organizing and managing data in a structured manner.

Tables: A table is the primary building block of a database. It consists of rows and columns, much like a spreadsheet, and stores data in a structured format. Each table should represent a unique entity, such as customers, products, or orders.

Columns (Fields): Columns, also known as fields, define the attributes or properties of the entities represented by a table. For example, a "Customers" table may have columns such as CustomerID, FirstName, LastName, Email, and Phone.

Rows (Records): Rows, also known as records, represent individual instances of the entities described by a table. Each row contains values for the columns defined in the table. For example, in the "Customers" table, a row might represent a specific customer with a unique CustomerID, FirstName, LastName, Email, and Phone.

Data Types: Each column in a table has an associated data type, which determines the kind of data that can be stored in that column. Common data types include integers, floating-point numbers, text, dates, and binary data. Choosing the appropriate data type for a column is essential for ensuring data integrity and optimizing storage space.

Keys: Keys are used to establish relationships between tables and enforce data integrity constraints. There are two main types of keys:
- Primary Key: A primary key is a unique identifier for each row in a table. It consists of one or more columns that uniquely identify a record. A table can have only one primary key, and its values must be unique and not null.
- Foreign Key: A foreign key is a column or set of columns in a table that refers to the primary key of another table. The purpose of a foreign key is to maintain referential integrity, ensuring that relationships between tables are consistent and that related data is not deleted or orphaned accidentally.

Indexes: Indexes are database objects that help improve data retrieval performance. They can be created on one or more columns in a table, allowing the database to find records more quickly when searching for specific values. Properly designed and implemented indexes can greatly improve query performance.

Views: A view is a virtual table that displays the result of a stored query. It provides a way to encapsulate complex queries or present a simplified representation of the underlying data. Views do not store data themselves but reference the data in the base tables.

Stored Procedures and Functions: Stored procedures and functions are precompiled SQL code that can be executed on demand. They allow for modular and reusable code, improving maintainability and reducing the complexity of SQL queries.

Now that you have a better understanding of the various components of a database, you are ready to create your first database using SQLite Studio. In the next section, we will learn through the process of creating a database, defining tables, and establishing relationships between tables.

Creating Your First Database

Creating your first database involves several steps, such as defining the database structure, creating tables, and establishing relationships between tables. In this section, we will discuss the process of creating a database and share some best practices to keep in mind.

Process and Best Practices

Define the Database Structure

Start by identifying the entities your database will represent and the relationships between them. For example, if you are creating a database for an e-commerce store, you may have entities like customers, products, and orders. Sketch an Entity-Relationship Diagram (ERD) to visualize the structure of your database and understand the relationships between entities.

Choose Appropriate Data Types

When creating tables, make sure to choose the correct data type for each column. This ensures data integrity and optimizes storage space. For example, use integers for numerical IDs, text for names, and dates for date-related information.

Normalize Your Database

Normalization is the process of organizing the database structure to minimize data redundancy and improve data integrity. This involves creating separate tables for each entity and establishing relationships between them using primary and foreign keys. Aim for at least Third Normal Form (3NF) when designing your database.

Define Primary Keys

Each table should have a primary key that uniquely identifies each row. Primary keys should be unique and not null. They can be single columns or composite keys (a combination of multiple columns). Consider using surrogate keys (system-generated unique identifiers) for primary keys when natural keys (column or set of columns that uniquely identify a row based on the data itself) are not suitable.

Establish Relationships Using Foreign Keys

Use foreign keys to establish relationships between tables and maintain referential integrity. A foreign key in one table refers to the primary key of another table, ensuring that related data is consistent and not accidentally deleted or orphaned.

Create Indexes for Performance

Create indexes on columns that are frequently used in search conditions and join operations. Indexes can significantly improve query performance by allowing the database to quickly locate records with specific values. However, keep in mind that excessive or poorly designed indexes can negatively impact performance, as they consume additional storage space and require maintenance during data modification operations.

Implement Views, Stored Procedures, and Functions

Use views to encapsulate complex queries or present a simplified representation of the underlying data. Implement stored procedures and functions for modular and reusable code, improving maintainability and reducing the complexity of SQL queries.

Plan for Scalability and Security

When designing your database, consider future growth and potential changes in requirements. Plan for scaling your database by partitioning large tables, optimizing queries, and implementing caching. Implement proper access controls and data encryption to protect sensitive data.

Test and Validate Your Database Design

Before deploying your database, test and validate your design to ensure it meets the requirements and performs well under expected workloads. Use sample data and realistic test scenarios to identify potential issues and optimize your database design.

Document Your Database Design

Finally, document your database design, including the structure, relationships, keys, indexes, and any other relevant information. This documentation will help you and your team understand, maintain, and extend your database in the future.

By following these best practices and keeping these points in mind, you will be better equipped to create a well-designed and efficient database. In the next section, we will walk you through creating a sample database using SQLite Studio.

My First Database using SQLite Studio

In this section, we'll walk you through the process of creating a sample database using SQLite Studio. We'll create a simple database to manage a library system, with tables for books, authors, and genres.

Create a New Database

- Launch SQLite Studio if you haven't already.

- Click on the "Database" menu at the top of the SQLite Studio window.

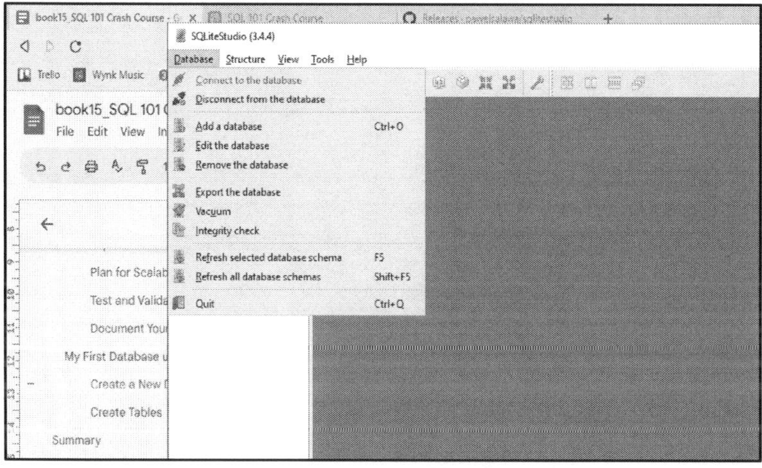

- Select "Add a database" from the dropdown menu.

- Choose a name for your new database, like "LibrarySystem", and select a location to save it.

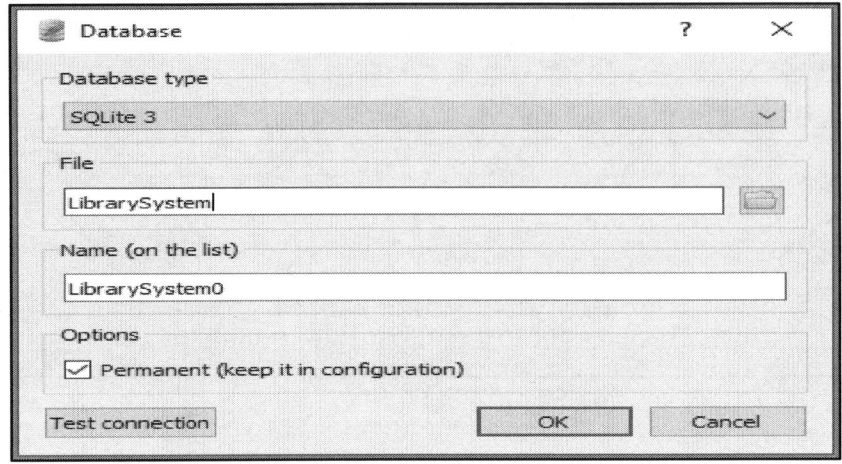

- Click "Save" to create the new database.

Create Tables

- Now, let us create the tables for our database.

- Create the "Authors" table:
    - Right-click on the newly created database (LibrarySystem) in the left panel and select "Create a table".
    - Name the table "Authors".

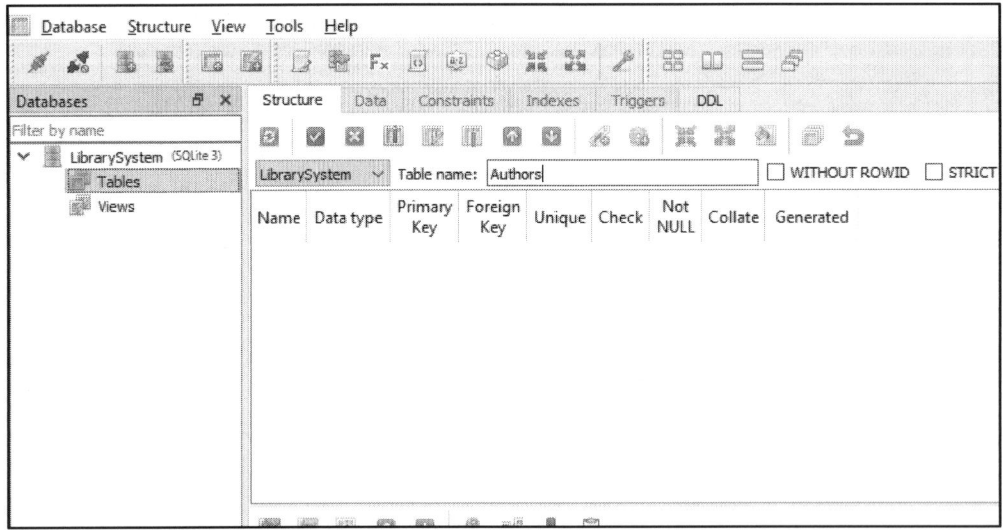

- Click on 'Add Column' as below:

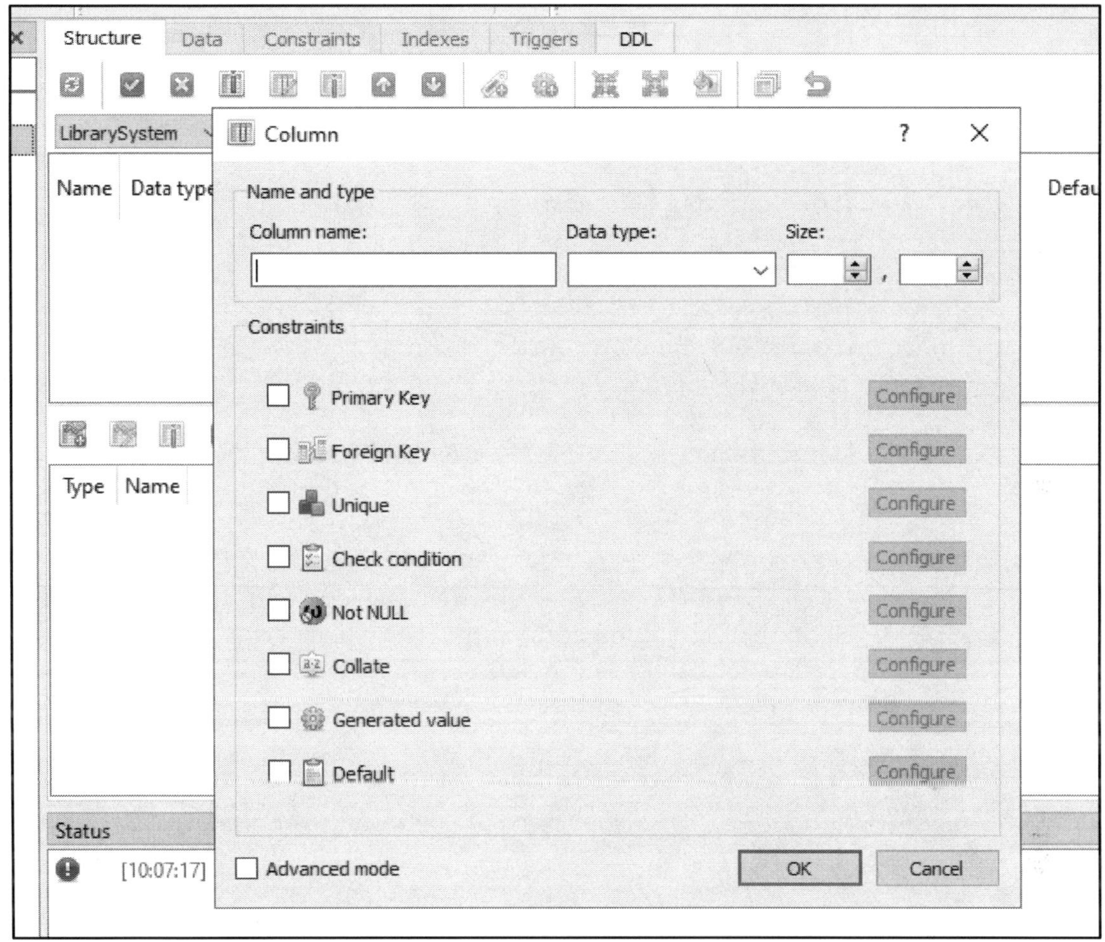

- Add the following columns:
    - AuthorID: INTEGER, Primary Key, Auto-increment
    - FirstName: TEXT, Not Null (check the "NN" checkbox)
    - LastName: TEXT, Not Null (check the "NN" checkbox)
    - Click on 'Commit Structure Changes' (press Ctrl + S)

- Create the "Genres" table:
    - Right-click on the database (LibrarySystem) in the left panel and select "Create a table".
    - Name the table "Genres".
    - Add the following columns:
    - GenreID: INTEGER, Primary Key, Auto-increment
    - GenreName: TEXT, Not Null, Unique (check the "NN" and "U" checkboxes)

- o   Click on 'Commit Structure Changes' (press Ctrl + S)

- Create the "Books" table:
    - o   Right-click on the database (LibrarySystem) in the left panel and select "Create a table".
    - o   Name the table "Books".
    - o   Add the following columns:
    - o   BookID: INTEGER, Primary Key, Auto-increment
    - o   Title: TEXT, Not Null (check the "NN" checkbox)
    - o   AuthorID: INTEGER, Foreign Key (check the "FK" checkbox and select the "Authors" table and "AuthorID" column)
    - o   GenreID: INTEGER, Foreign Key (check the "FK" checkbox and select the "Genres" table and "GenreID" column)
    - o   PublicationYear: INTEGER, Not Null (check the "NN" checkbox)
    - o   Click on 'Commit Structure Changes' (press Ctrl + S)

- Add Sample Data (Optional)
    - o   Right-click on a table (e.g., Authors) in the left panel and select "Open table".
    - o   Click on the "+" button at the top of the table view to add a new row.
    - o   Enter data for each column and press Enter or click outside the row to save the changes.

Following the above step-by-step instructions, you have successfully created your first database using SQLite Studio. The database should look like as below:

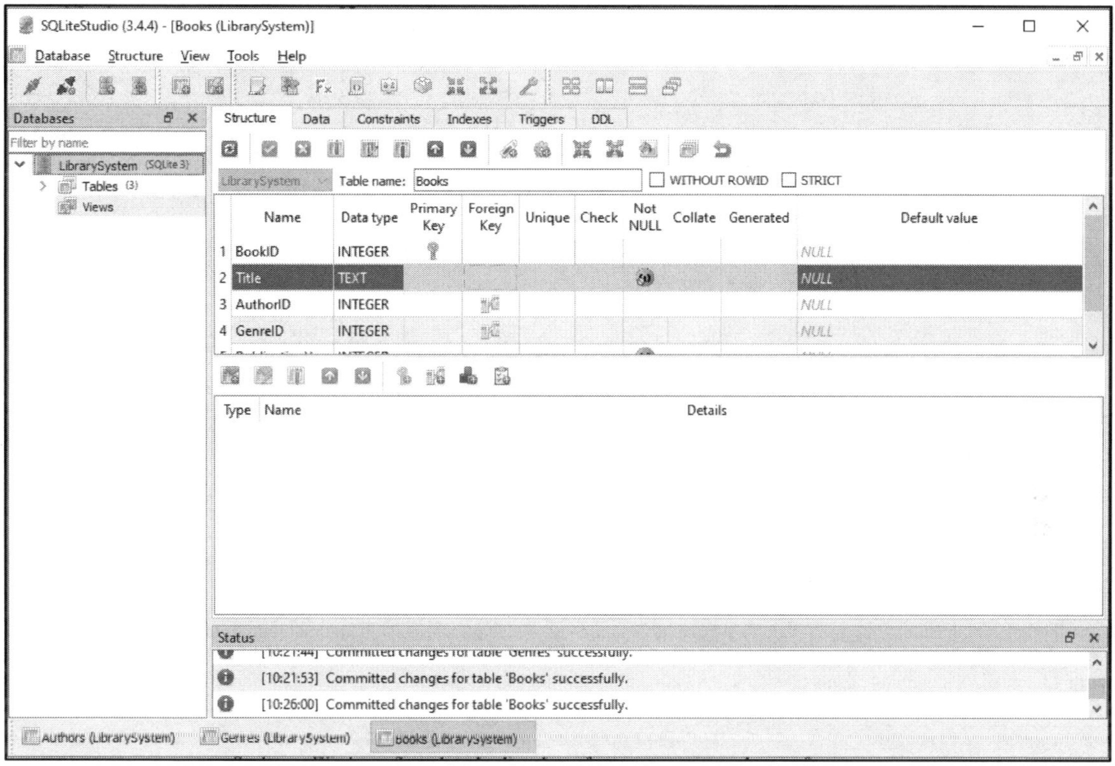

Summary

In this chapter, we covered the process of setting up your SQL environment, creating your first database using SQLite Studio, and understanding the structure of a database. We began by discussing the importance of using a SQL tool and introduced SQLite Studio, a powerful and user-friendly tool for managing SQLite databases. We highlighted its features, including its intuitive interface, syntax highlighting, autocompletion, and more.

We then walked you through the step-by-step process of installing and setting up SQLite Studio on Windows, from downloading the software to creating a shortcut for easy access. After setting up SQLite Studio, we delved into the structure of a database, explaining the various components such as databases, tables, columns, rows, data types, keys, indexes, views, stored procedures, and functions. This understanding of the database structure is crucial for creating well-designed and efficient databases. We also discussed the process of creating a database and shared some best practices to keep in mind, such as defining the database structure, choosing appropriate data types, normalizing the database, defining primary and foreign keys, creating indexes, implementing views and stored procedures, planning for scalability and security, testing and validating the design, and documenting the database structure.

Finally, we walked you through creating a sample database for a library system using SQLite Studio. We created tables for authors, genres, and books, and established relationships between the tables using primary and foreign keys. Optionally, we added sample data to the tables, providing a foundation for practicing SQL queries and exploring database management further.

CHAPTER 3: SQL QUERIES BASICS

In this comprehensive chapter, we aim to equip SQL developers with a solid foundation of essential SQL queries that are crucial for their day-to-day work. We will delve into the details of each SQL query statement, breaking down the syntax, semantics, and various components involved. By examining real-world applications, we will demonstrate the practical utility of these queries, helping developers understand when and how to apply them effectively.

Utilizing an SQLite database as our primary example, we will walk you through the process of implementing these SQL queries, ensuring a smooth and seamless experience. By focusing on the most widely used SQL commands, such as SELECT, INSERT, UPDATE, DELETE, JOIN, and GROUP BY, we will help developers build a strong command of the language and boost their productivity in managing databases.

Create Sample Database

To begin the process, we will create an additional straightforward dataset for each table, akin to what was described in the previous example. By constructing these new datasets, we can further explore the functionalities and applications of our data processing methods. This will involve generating sample data, organizing it into a coherent format, and then inputting it into the respective tables. By doing this, we can ensure a better understanding of the techniques and principles discussed, while also gaining practical experience in data manipulation and management.

The dataset consists of two tables: customers and orders.

Customers Table:

customer_id	first_name	last_name	email
1	John	Doe	john.doe@example.com
2	Jane	Smith	jane.smith@example.com
3	Alice	Johnson	alice.johnson@example.com

Orders Table:

order_id	customer_id	product_id	price	quantity	created_at
1	1	1	10	5	2023-01-01 12:00:00
2	2	2	20	10	2023-01-15 16:00:00
3	3	3	30	20	2023-02-05 10:00:00

Follow these step-by-step instructions to create the database, tables, and columns in SQLite Studio:

Open SQLite Studio.

Click on the "New Database" icon in the toolbar or choose "Add a new database" from the File menu.

Choose a location to save the database file, and give it a name, such as "example.db".

Click "Save" to create the new database.

Create Tables

Create the customers table:
- Right-click the newly created database in the "Databases" panel and choose "Create a table".
-
- In the "Table name" field, enter "customers".
-
- Click on the "Add a column" button (green plus icon) to create columns.
-
- For each column, enter the name, data type, and constraints:
    - Column 1: Name - "customer_id", Type - INTEGER, check the "Primary Key" and "Not NULL" constraints.
    - Column 2: Name - "first_name", Type - TEXT, check the "Not NULL" constraint.
    - Column 3: Name - "last_name", Type - TEXT, check the "Not NULL" constraint.
    - Column 4: Name - "email", Type - TEXT, check the "Not NULL" constraint.
- Click "OK" to create the customers table.

Create the orders table:
- Right-click the database in the "Databases" panel and choose "Create a table".
- In the "Table name" field, enter "orders".
- Click on the "Add a column" button (green plus icon) to create columns.
- For each column, enter the name, data type, and constraints:
    - Column 1: Name - "order_id", Type - INTEGER, check the "Primary Key" and "Not NULL" constraints.
    - Column 2: Name - "customer_id", Type - INTEGER, check the "Not NULL" constraint.

      ○ Column 3: Name - "product_id", Type - INTEGER, check the "Not NULL" constraint.
      ○ Column 4: Name - "price", Type - REAL, check the "Not NULL" constraint.
      ○ Column 5: Name - "quantity", Type - INTEGER, check the "Not NULL" constraint.
      ○ Column 6: Name - "created_at", Type - DATETIME, check the "Not NULL" constraint.
- Click "OK" to create the orders table.

Now that we have both tables created, let us insert the example data into these tables:

Insert Data

Insert data into the customers table:
- In SQLite Studio, click on the "New SQL Editor" button in the toolbar or choose "Open SQL Editor" from the "File" menu.
- In the SQL Editor, enter the following SQL queries to insert data into the customers table:

```
INSERT INTO customers (customer_id, first_name, last_name, email)
VALUES (1, 'John', 'Doe', 'john.doe@example.com');


INSERT INTO customers (customer_id, first_name, last_name, email)
VALUES (2, 'Jane', 'Smith', 'jane.smith@example.com');


INSERT INTO customers (customer_id, first_name, last_name, email)
VALUES (3, 'Alice', 'Johnson', 'alice.johnson@example.com');
```

- Click "Execute SQL" (F9) to run the queries and insert the data.

Insert data into the orders table:

```
INSERT INTO orders (order_id, customer_id, product_id, price, quantity,
created_at)
VALUES (1, 1, 1, 10, 5, '2023-01-01 12:00:00');


INSERT INTO orders (order_id, customer_id, product_id, price, quantity,
```

created_at)
VALUES (2, 2, 2, 20, 10, '2023-01-15 16:00:00');

INSERT INTO orders (order_id, customer_id, product_id, price, quantity,
created_at)
VALUES (3, 3, 3, 30, 20, '2023-02-05 10:00:00');

- Click "Execute SQL" (F9) to run the queries and insert the data.

In case, if you encounter issues with executing multiple queries, write one query at a time, execute it, then clear the SQL editor and write another query. For example,

- In the SQL Editor, write the first SQL query for inserting data into the customers table:

INSERT INTO customers (customer_id, first_name, last_name, email)
VALUES (1, 'John', 'Doe', 'john.doe@example.com');

- Click "Execute SQL" (F9) or the "Execute" button in the toolbar to run the query and insert the data.

- Clear the SQL Editor or open a new SQL Editor, and write the second SQL query for inserting data into the customers table. Repeat the same process for inserting data into the orders table. By executing the queries individually, you should be able to insert all the rows without any issues.

Now you have successfully created the example database, tables, and columns in SQLite Studio and inserted the example data into the tables. The data should appear like this:

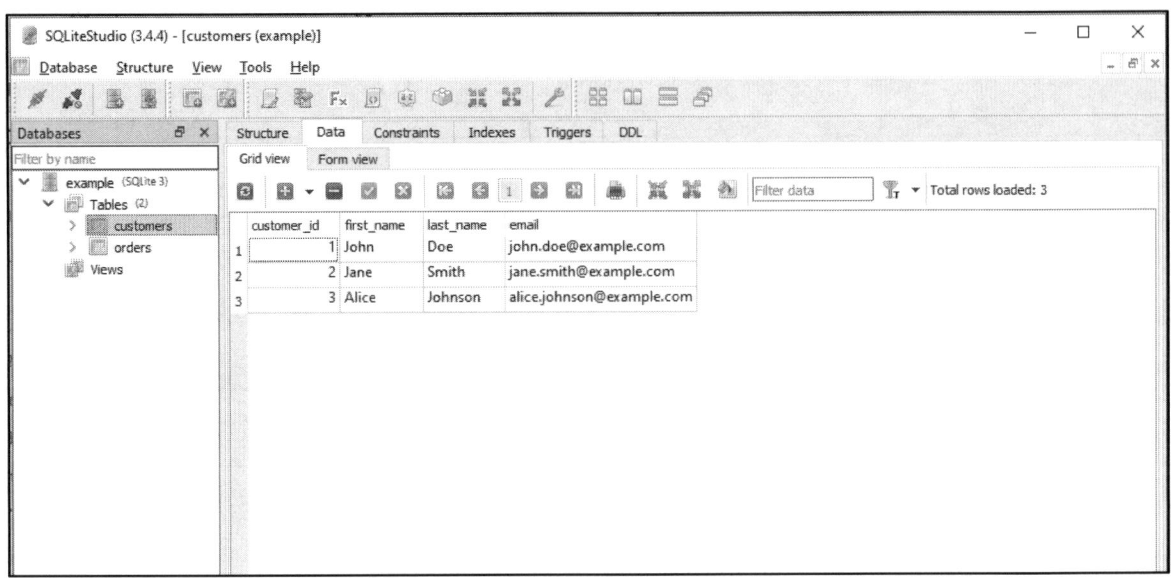

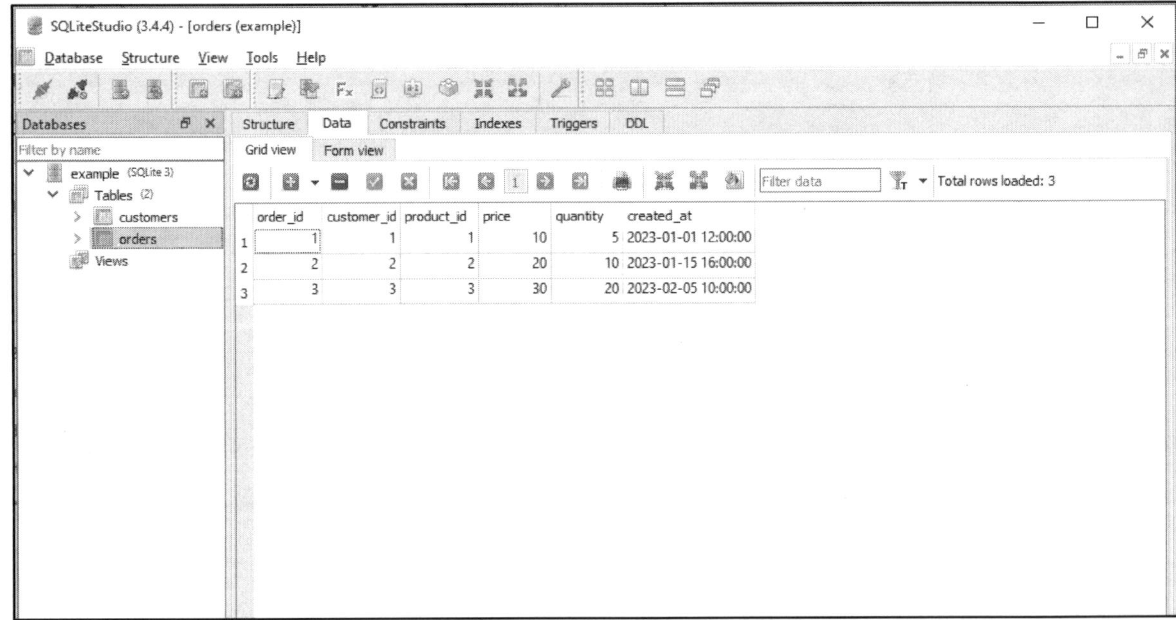

You can now use this database to practice SQL queries and analyze the data. The database is alternatively available to download from our official github repository: https://github.com/kittenpub/database-repository/blob/main/example.db

Now, let us dive into the essential SQL queries:

SELECT Statement

The SELECT statement is used to retrieve data from one or more tables. It allows you to specify the columns to be retrieved, conditions for filtering data, and the order in which the data should be displayed. We will cover the basics of the SELECT statement, including projections, filters, sorting, and combining results from multiple tables using JOINs.

Suppose we want to retrieve a list of all customers from the customers table. We can use the SELECT statement as follows:

```
SELECT * FROM customers;
```

In the above code snippet, the asterisk (*) represents all columns in the table. To retrieve specific columns, you can list them after the SELECT keyword:

```
SELECT first_name, last_name, email FROM customers;
```

INSERT Statement

The INSERT statement is used to add new rows to a table. We will discuss how to insert a single row, multiple rows, or rows from another table using the INSERT statement. Additionally, we will cover the use of default values and the RETURNING clause for returning the inserted data.

To insert a new customer into the customers table, use the INSERT statement:

```
INSERT INTO customers (first_name, last_name, email, country) VALUES ('John', 'Doe', 'john.doe@example.com', 'USA');
```

UPDATE Statement

The UPDATE statement is used to modify existing rows in a table. We will explore how to update one or more columns of a row or multiple rows based on specified conditions. We will also discuss the importance of the WHERE clause in preventing unintentional updates and the use of the RETURNING clause to return the updated data.

To update the email address of a specific customer, use the UPDATE statement with a WHERE clause:

```
UPDATE customers SET email = 'john.doe_new@example.com' WHERE
first_name = 'John' AND last_name = 'Doe';
```

DELETE Statement

The DELETE statement is used to remove rows from a table. We will explain how to delete a single row, multiple rows, or all rows in a table based on specified conditions. We will emphasize the importance of the WHERE clause in preventing unintentional deletions and the use of the RETURNING clause to return the deleted data.

To delete a customer from the customers table, use the DELETE statement with a WHERE clause:

```
DELETE FROM customers WHERE first_name = 'John' AND last_name = 'Doe';
```

Transaction Control

In this section, we will cover the basics of transaction control, explaining the concepts of commit, rollback, and savepoints. We will demonstrate how to use these commands to manage transactions in SQL and ensure data consistency and integrity.

To start a transaction, use the BEGIN TRANSACTION command:

```
BEGIN TRANSACTION;
```

Data Definition Language (DDL)

DDL statements are used to define and manage the structure of your database, such as creating, altering, and dropping tables, indexes, and views. We will discuss the CREATE TABLE, ALTER TABLE, DROP TABLE, CREATE INDEX, DROP INDEX, CREATE VIEW, and DROP VIEW statements.

To create a new table, use the CREATE TABLE statement:

```
CREATE TABLE new_table (
   id INTEGER PRIMARY KEY,
   name TEXT NOT NULL
);
```

To add a new column to an existing table, use the ALTER TABLE statement:

```
ALTER TABLE new_table ADD COLUMN email TEXT;
```

To delete a table, use the DROP TABLE statement:

```
DROP TABLE new_table;
```

Data Manipulation Language (DML)

DML statements are used to insert, update, and delete data in your database. We have already discussed the INSERT, UPDATE, and DELETE statements in detail. In this section, we will explore advanced techniques and best practices for working with these statements.

Now that you have learned the basic DML statements (INSERT, UPDATE, DELETE), you can combine them with other SQL features such as subqueries, functions, and operators to create more complex queries.

For example, to update the email address of all customers from a specific country, you can use a subquery in the WHERE clause:

```
UPDATE customers
SET email = REPLACE(email, '@example.com', '@newexample.com')
WHERE country = (SELECT country FROM countries WHERE country_name =
'USA');
```

ORDER BY Clause

The ORDER BY clause is used to sort the result of a SELECT statement based on one or more columns in either ascending (ASC) or descending (DESC) order. By default, if neither ASC nor DESC is specified, the results will be sorted in ascending order.

For the given SQLite database, let us explore some examples to understand the use of the ORDER BY clause.

Sorting by a single column:

Suppose we want to retrieve a list of all customers from the customers table, sorted by their last name. We can use the SELECT statement with the ORDER BY clause as follows:

```
SELECT first_name, last_name, email FROM customers ORDER BY last_name;
```

This will sort the results by the last_name column in ascending order. If you want to sort the results in descending order, add the DESC keyword:

```
SELECT first_name, last_name, email FROM customers ORDER BY last_name DESC;
```

Sorting by multiple columns:

You can also sort the results by multiple columns by specifying a comma-separated list of columns in the ORDER BY clause. The results will be sorted by the first column, and in case of ties, they will be sorted by the next column in the list, and so on.

For example, if you want to retrieve a list of all customers, sorted first by their country and then by their last name within each country, you can use the following query:

```
SELECT first_name, last_name, email, country FROM customers ORDER BY country, last_name;
```

This will sort the results first by the country column in ascending order and then by the last_name column in ascending order within each country.

Combining ORDER BY with other clauses:

You can combine the ORDER BY clause with other SQL clauses, such as WHERE and LIMIT, to create more specific queries.

For example, if you want to retrieve the top 5 customers from the USA, sorted by their last name in descending order, you can use the following query:

```
SELECT first_name, last_name, email FROM customers WHERE country = 'USA' ORDER BY last_name DESC LIMIT 5;
```

In this query, the WHERE clause filters the customers by their country, the ORDER BY clause sorts the results by the last_name column in descending order, and the LIMIT clause limits the results to the first 5 records.

LIMIT and OFFSET

The LIMIT and OFFSET clauses are used in conjunction with the SELECT statement to limit the number of rows returned by a query and to specify the starting point for the returned rows, respectively. These clauses are particularly useful when you want to retrieve a specific range of rows, such as when implementing pagination in an application.

LIMIT

The LIMIT clause is used to restrict the number of rows returned by a query. It takes an integer value as an argument, which represents the maximum number of rows to return.

For example, if you want to retrieve the top 3 customers from the customers table, sorted by their last name, you can use the following query:

```
SELECT first_name, last_name, email FROM customers ORDER BY last_name LIMIT 3;
```

This query will return only the first 3 rows from the sorted result.

OFFSET

The OFFSET clause is used to specify the starting point for the rows returned by a query. It takes an integer value as an argument, which represents the number of rows to skip before starting to return rows.

For example, if you want to retrieve customers 6 through 10 from the customers table, sorted by their last name, you can use the following query:

```
SELECT first_name, last_name, email FROM customers ORDER BY last_name LIMIT 5 OFFSET 5;
```

In this query, the OFFSET clause skips the first 5 rows, and the LIMIT clause returns the next 5 rows (rows 6 to 10) from the sorted result.

Combining LIMIT and OFFSET

You can combine the LIMIT and OFFSET clauses to retrieve a specific range of rows from a query.

The general syntax is:

```
SELECT column1, column2, ... FROM table_name ORDER BY column_name
[ASC | DESC] LIMIT number_of_rows OFFSET starting_row;
```

For example, to retrieve customers 11 through 20 from the customers table, sorted by their last name, you can use the following query:

```
SELECT first_name, last_name, email FROM customers ORDER BY last_name
LIMIT 10 OFFSET 10;
```

In this query, the OFFSET clause skips the first 10 rows, and the LIMIT clause returns the next 10 rows (rows 11 to 20) from the sorted result.

Filtering Results

Filtering results in SQL is an essential technique for retrieving specific data that meets certain criteria. You can use various clauses and operators in conjunction with the SELECT statement to filter the results based on specific conditions.

WHERE Clause

The WHERE clause is used to filter data based on specific conditions. It allows you to use comparison operators, logical operators, and functions to define the conditions.

For example, if you want to retrieve customers from the customers table who live in the USA, you can use the following query:

```
SELECT first_name, last_name, email FROM customers WHERE country = 'USA';
```

Comparison Operators

Comparison operators are used to compare values and include equal to (=), not equal to (<> or !=), greater than (>), less than (<), greater than or equal to (>=), and less than or equal to (<=).

For example, if you want to retrieve customers with an account balance greater than 1000, you can use the following query:

```
SELECT first_name, last_name, email, account_balance FROM customers WHERE
account_balance > 1000;
```

Logical Operators

Logical operators are used to combine multiple conditions and include AND, OR, and NOT.

For example, if you want to retrieve customers from the USA with an account balance greater than 1000, you can use the AND operator:

```
SELECT first_name, last_name, email, account_balance FROM customers WHERE country = 'USA' AND account_balance > 1000;
```

If you want to retrieve customers from the USA or customers with an account balance greater than 1000, you can use the OR operator:

```
SELECT first_name, last_name, email, account_balance FROM customers WHERE country = 'USA' OR account_balance > 1000;
```

If you want to retrieve customers who are not from the USA, you can use the NOT operator:

```
SELECT first_name, last_name, email FROM customers WHERE NOT country = 'USA';
```

Functions

You can use SQL functions to filter results based on specific conditions. Functions can be used to perform calculations, manipulate strings, work with dates and times, and more.

For example, if you want to retrieve customers with email addresses from a specific domain, you can use the LIKE operator with the '%' wildcard character:

```
SELECT first_name, last_name, email FROM customers WHERE email LIKE '%@example.com';
```

Combining Filtering Techniques

You can combine various filtering techniques to create complex queries that return specific data.

For example, if you want to retrieve customers from the USA with an account balance greater than 1000 and an email address from a specific domain, you can use the following query:

```
SELECT first_name, last_name, email, account_balance FROM customers WHERE
country = 'USA' AND account_balance > 1000 AND email LIKE
'%@example.com';
```

SQL Query Best Practices

Using SQL queries effectively and efficiently is essential for any SQL developer. The given below are some best practices to help you get the most out of your basic SQL queries:

Be Specific with SELECT Columns

Instead of using the SELECT * syntax to select all columns, specify the columns you need in your query. This helps reduce the amount of data returned and improves query performance.

```
-- Good practice
SELECT first_name, last_name, email FROM customers;
```

```
-- Not recommended
SELECT * FROM customers;
```

Use Meaningful Aliases

When using aliases for tables or columns, choose names that are clear and meaningful. This makes your query more readable and easier to understand.

```
-- Good practice
SELECT c.first_name, c.last_name, o.order_date FROM customers c JOIN orders o
ON c.customer_id = o.customer_id;
```

```
-- Not recommended
SELECT a.first_name, a.last_name, b.order_date FROM customers a JOIN orders b
ON a.customer_id = b.customer_id;
```

Use Appropriate Filtering Techniques

Always use the appropriate filtering techniques, such as the WHERE clause and comparison operators, to narrow down the data returned by your query. This helps improve query performance and makes your results more relevant.

-- Good practice

```sql
SELECT first_name, last_name, email FROM customers WHERE country = 'USA'
AND account_balance > 1000;
```

-- Not recommended

```sql
SELECT first_name, last_name, email FROM customers;
```

Limit the Number of Rows Returned

When you don't need all rows from a query, use the LIMIT clause to restrict the number of rows returned. This helps improve query performance and reduces the amount of data processed by your application.

-- Good practice

```sql
SELECT first  name, last  name, email FROM customers ORDER BY last_name
LIMIT 10;
```

-- Not recommended

```sql
SELECT first_name, last_name, email FROM customers ORDER BY last_name;
```

Optimize JOINs:

When using JOINs, try to use the appropriate type of join (e.g., INNER JOIN, OUTER JOIN) and ensure that you're joining on indexed columns. This helps improve query performance.

-- Good practice

```sql
SELECT c.first_name, c.last_name, o.order_date FROM customers c INNER JOIN
orders o ON c.customer_id = o.customer_id;
```

-- Not recommended (assuming customer_id is an indexed column)

```sql
SELECT c.first_name, c.last_name, o.order_date FROM customers c INNER JOIN
orders o ON c.email = o.customer_email;
```

Use Comments

Add comments to your SQL queries to explain the purpose of the query, any assumptions made, or any complex logic. This helps improve the readability and maintainability of your code.

-- Good practice

```sql
-- Retrieve customers from the USA with an account balance greater than 1000
SELECT first_name, last_name, email, account_balance FROM customers WHERE
country = 'USA' AND account_balance > 1000;
```

Format Queries

Use consistent formatting and indentation in your SQL queries. This helps improve the readability of your code and makes it easier to understand.

-- Good practice

```sql
SELECT c.first_name,
    c.last_name,
    o.order_date
FROM customers c
INNER JOIN orders o ON c.customer_id = o.customer_id;
```

By following these best practices, you can write efficient and maintainable SQL queries that effectively retrieve and analyze data from your database. Practicing these techniques on the provided SQLite database will help you become a more proficient SQL developer.

Summary

In this chapter, we delved into the basics of SQL queries, focusing on essential SQL statements and clauses that every SQL developer must know and be proficient with. We began by providing an overview of key SQL queries and then dove deeper into each one, illustrating their usage with a provided SQLite database.

We learned about the SELECT statement, which is used to retrieve data from one or more tables, specifying the columns to be retrieved and filtering the data based on certain conditions. We discussed the importance of being specific with SELECT columns, using meaningful aliases, and optimizing JOINs for better query performance. We explored various filtering techniques using the WHERE clause, comparison operators, logical operators, and SQL functions. We discovered how these techniques can be combined to create complex queries that return specific data based on multiple conditions. We also discussed the use of the ORDER BY clause to sort query results based on one or more columns in ascending or descending order.

Next, we covered the LIMIT and OFFSET clauses, which help restrict the number of rows returned by a query and specify the starting point for the returned rows. These clauses are particularly useful when retrieving specific ranges of rows, such as when implementing pagination in an application. Additionally, we shared some best practices for writing efficient and maintainable SQL queries, such as using comments, consistent formatting, and choosing the appropriate filtering techniques. By following these best practices, developers can create better-performing queries and improve the overall efficiency of their applications.

Throughout the chapter, we provided examples and step-by-step instructions for applying these SQL queries and concepts to a given SQLite database. By understanding and practicing these fundamental SQL query techniques, readers will be well-equipped to analyze data effectively and build more efficient applications. The knowledge gained in this chapter lays the foundation for more advanced SQL topics covered in subsequent chapters, helping readers become skilled SQL developers.

Chapter 4: Turning Data into Information

In this chapter, we delve into the critical process of converting raw data into valuable information and explore the powerful role SQL plays in achieving this objective. We will provide a comprehensive overview of essential topics, including the GROUP BY clause, which enables data organization based on specific attributes, and the HAVING clause, which allows for filtering groups according to defined conditions. Furthermore, we will discuss the indispensable role of aggregate functions, such as COUNT, SUM, AVG, MIN, and MAX, which facilitate complex data analysis and empower us to transform vast quantities of data into actionable insights. By mastering these essential SQL components, one can unlock the true potential of their data, derive meaningful patterns, and drive strategic decision-making, ultimately leading to improved business outcomes and growth. The chapter aims to provide a solid foundation for harnessing the power of SQL to turn raw data into valuable business intelligence.

Overview of SQL Techniques

Data stored in databases often consists of vast amounts of records, making it challenging to derive valuable insights directly from the raw data. SQL provides various techniques to process, analyze, and manipulate the data, enabling us to convert raw data into meaningful information that can be used for decision-making, reporting, and optimization.

Some key techniques in SQL that help in turning data into information are:

GROUP BY Clause

The GROUP BY clause allows you to group rows in a table based on one or more columns. This is particularly useful when you want to perform calculations or aggregate data on specific groups of rows. For example, you can use the GROUP BY clause to find the total sales for each product category or the average salary for each department.

Aggregate Functions

Aggregate functions perform calculations on a set of values and return a single value. Common aggregate functions include COUNT, SUM, AVG, MIN, and MAX. These functions can be used in conjunction with the GROUP BY clause to perform calculations on each group of rows. For instance, you can calculate the total revenue for each region or the highest salary for each job title.

HAVING Clause

The HAVING clause is used to filter the results of a GROUP BY query based on a condition that involves an aggregate function. This allows you to retrieve groups that meet specific criteria, such as finding products with an average rating above a certain threshold or departments with a total salary above a certain amount.

In the following sections of this chapter, we'll dive deeper into these topics and learn how to use these techniques effectively to extract valuable information from raw data. We'll provide practical examples and step-by-step instructions to help you master these concepts and become proficient in turning data into meaningful insights using SQL.

Aggregating Data with GROUP BY

The GROUP BY clause is used to group rows with the same values in specified columns into a single row, allowing you to perform aggregate functions on each group. Aggregate functions, such as COUNT, SUM, AVG, MIN, and MAX, can be applied to each group of rows to perform calculations and analyze data.

Let us explore through the steps to use the GROUP BY clause along with aggregate functions using the provided SQLite database:
https://github.com/kittenpub/database-repository/blob/main/example.db

Examine 'orders' Table Structure

First, import the database and take a look at the 'orders' table. It contains information about each order, such as the 'order_id', 'customer_id', 'product_id', 'quantity', and 'order_date'.

Group Data by Specific Column

To group data by a specific column, use the GROUP BY clause followed by the column name(s). For example, if you want to group the orders by the 'product_id', the query would look like this:

```
SELECT product_id
FROM orders
GROUP BY product_id;
```

Apply Aggregate Functions

Now, let us assume that you want to calculate the total quantity ordered for each product. You can use the SUM() function along with the GROUP BY clause:

```
SELECT product_id, SUM(quantity) as total_quantity
FROM orders
```

```
GROUP BY product_id;
```

This query will return the total quantity ordered for each product in the 'orders' table.

Group Data by Multiple Columns

You can also group data by multiple columns. For example, if you want to group the orders by both 'customer_id' and 'product_id', the query would look like this:

```
SELECT customer_id, product_id, SUM(quantity) as total_quantity
FROM orders
GROUP BY customer_id, product_id;
```

This query will return the total quantity ordered for each combination of customer and product.

Remember to practice using the GROUP BY clause with different aggregate functions and column combinations to become more proficient in turning data into valuable information.

HAVING Clause

The HAVING clause is used in conjunction with the GROUP BY clause to filter the results of a query based on a condition that involves an aggregate function. It allows you to retrieve groups that meet specific criteria. The HAVING clause is similar to the WHERE clause, but it works on the results of grouped data rather than individual rows.

Basic Structure of HAVING Clause

The basic structure of a query using the HAVING clause is as follows:

```
SELECT column(s), aggregate_function(column)
FROM table
GROUP BY column(s)
HAVING condition;
```

Example

Consider the 'orders' table from the database. Suppose you want to find the products with a total quantity ordered greater than a specific threshold, say 100. You can use the HAVING clause along with the GROUP BY clause and the SUM() function:

```
SELECT product_id, SUM(quantity) as total_quantity
FROM orders
GROUP BY product_id
HAVING total_quantity > 100;
```

This query will return the product IDs and their total quantities ordered for those products with a total quantity greater than 100.

Using Multiple Conditions

You can also use multiple conditions in the HAVING clause by combining them with logical operators like AND, OR, and NOT. For instance, if you want to find the products with a total quantity ordered between 50 and 100, you can use the following query:

```
SELECT product_id, SUM(quantity) as total_quantity
FROM orders
GROUP BY product_id
HAVING total_quantity >= 50 AND total_quantity <= 100;
```

This query will return the product IDs and their total quantities ordered for those products with a total quantity between 50 and 100.

By using the HAVING clause along with the GROUP BY clause and aggregate functions, you can filter and analyze grouped data based on specific conditions. Do not forget to practice using the HAVING clause with different aggregate functions, conditions, and logical operators on the provided SQLite database to further enhance your data analysis skills.

COUNT, SUM, AVG, MIN, MAX

Aggregate functions are used to perform calculations on a set of values and return a single value. These functions can be used with the GROUP BY clause to analyze and aggregate grouped data. The most common aggregate functions are COUNT, SUM, AVG, MIN, and MAX.

COUNT

The COUNT() function returns the number of rows in a group or a table. For example, to find the total number of orders for each product, you can use the following query:

```
SELECT product_id, COUNT(order_id) as total_orders
FROM orders
GROUP BY product_id;
```

SUM

The SUM() function calculates the sum of the specified column for each group. For example, to find the total quantity ordered for each product, you can use the following query:

```
SELECT product_id, SUM(quantity) as total_quantity
FROM orders
GROUP BY product_id;
```

AVG

The AVG() function calculates the average value of the specified column for each group. For instance, to find the average quantity ordered for each product, you can use the following query:

```
SELECT product_id, AVG(quantity) as average_quantity
FROM orders
GROUP BY product_id;
```

MIN

The MIN() function returns the minimum value of the specified column for each group. For example, to find the minimum quantity ordered for each product, you can use the following query:

```
SELECT product_id, MIN(quantity) as min_quantity
FROM orders
GROUP BY product_id;
```

MAX:

The MAX() function returns the maximum value of the specified column for each group. For instance, to find the maximum quantity ordered for each product, you can use the following query:

```
SELECT product_id, MAX(quantity) as max_quantity
FROM orders
GROUP BY product_id;
```

By using aggregate functions along with the GROUP BY clause, you can perform various calculations and analyses on your data. Be sure to practice using different aggregate functions and column combinations on the provided SQLite database.

Calculated Fields

Calculated fields are fields derived from existing columns in a table by applying mathematical or logical operations. They allow you to create new columns in the result set without modifying the original table. You can use arithmetic operators (+, -, *, /) and functions to create calculated fields.

Let us explore calculated fields using the provided SQLite database:
https://github.com/kittenpub/database-repository/blob/main/example.db

Examine 'orders' Table Structure

First, import the database and take a look at the 'orders' table. It contains information about each order, such as the 'order_id', 'customer_id', 'product_id', 'quantity', 'price', and 'order_date'.

Example of Calculated Field

Suppose you want to calculate the total price for each order by multiplying the 'quantity' and 'price' columns. You can create a calculated field called 'total_price' using the following query:

```
SELECT order_id, customer_id, product_id, quantity, price, quantity * price as
total_price
FROM orders;
```

The output for the given example.db file would look like this:

order_id	customer_id	product_id	quantity	price	total_price
1	1	1	2	10	20
2	1	2	1	15	15
3	2	1	3	10	30

Example with Mathematical Function

If you want to calculate the discounted price for each order by applying a 10% discount, you can use the following query:

```sql
SELECT order_id, customer_id, product_id, quantity, price, quantity * price * 0.9 as discounted_price
FROM orders;
```

The output for the given example.db file would look like this:

order_id	customer_id	product_id	quantity	price	discounted_price
1	1	1	2	10	18
2	1	2	1	15	13.5
3	2	1	3	10	27

Calculated fields can be used to perform various calculations and create new columns in your query results. Be sure to practice creating calculated fields using different arithmetic operations and functions on the provided SQLite database to become more proficient in transforming data into useful information.

Aliases

Aliases in SQL are used to temporarily rename a table or column for the purpose of a specific query. They can make your query more readable and easier to understand, especially when dealing with complex queries or joining multiple tables. Aliases can be assigned using the AS keyword or simply by providing the alias name after the column or table name.

Let us explore aliases using the provided SQLite database:
https://github.com/kittenpub/database-repository/blob/main/example.db

Column Aliases

Column aliases are used to rename a column in the result set. For example, if you want to rename the 'price' column to 'unit_price', you can use the following query:

```
SELECT order_id, customer_id, product_id, quantity, price AS unit_price
FROM orders;
```

Or, without using the AS keyword:

```
SELECT order_id, customer_id, product_id, quantity, price unit_price
FROM orders;
```

The output for the given example.db file would look like this:

order_id	customer_id	product_id	quantity	unit_price
1	1	1	2	10
2	1	2	1	15
3	2	1	3	10

Table Aliases

Table aliases are used to rename a table in a query, making it easier to reference when working with multiple tables. For example, let us assume you have another table named 'products' with columns 'product_id', 'product_name', and 'category'. If you want to join the 'orders' and 'products' tables and use aliases to make the query more readable, you can use the following query:

```
SELECT o.order_id, o.customer_id, p.product_id, p.product_name, o.quantity,
o.price
FROM orders AS o
JOIN products AS p
ON o.product_id = p.product_id;
```

Or, without using the AS keyword:

```sql
SELECT o.order_id, o.customer_id, p.product_id, p.product_name, o.quantity,
o.price
FROM orders o
JOIN products p
ON o.product_id = p.product_id;
```

In the above code snippet, 'o' is an alias for the 'orders' table, and 'p' is an alias for the 'products' table. The query is more readable with aliases, making it easier to understand the relationship between the tables.

Using aliases can help simplify and improve the readability of your SQL queries, particularly when working with complex queries or multiple tables. Practice using aliases with different tables and columns on the provided SQLite database to enhance your query-writing skills.

Handling NULL Values

In SQL, NULL values represent missing or unknown data. When working with databases, it's common to encounter NULL values, and it's essential to understand how to handle them. NULL values can cause unexpected results in your queries if not handled properly. Let us explore how to work with NULL values in SQL.

IS NULL and IS NOT NULL

When filtering data, you can use the IS NULL and IS NOT NULL operators to check for NULL values. These operators are used in the WHERE clause to filter rows based on the presence or absence of NULL values.

For example, to find all rows with a NULL value in the 'price' column:

```sql
SELECT * FROM orders
WHERE price IS NULL;
```

To find all rows without a NULL value in the 'price' column:

```sql
SELECT * FROM orders
WHERE price IS NOT NULL;
```

COALESCE

The COALESCE() function is used to return the first non-NULL value from a list of expressions. If all expressions evaluate to NULL, COALESCE() returns NULL.

For example, to display a default value of 0 when the 'price' column contains a NULL value:

```
SELECT order_id, customer_id, product_id, quantity, COALESCE(price, 0) AS price
FROM orders;
```

NULLIF

The NULLIF() function returns NULL if the two expressions provided as arguments are equal; otherwise, it returns the first expression. This can be useful when you want to convert a specific value to NULL.

For example, to replace any 'price' value of -1 with NULL:

```
SELECT order_id, customer_id, product_id, quantity, NULLIF(price, -1) AS price
FROM orders;
```

Handling NULL Values in Aggregate Functions

Aggregate functions (COUNT, SUM, AVG, MIN, and MAX) generally ignore NULL values. However, the COUNT function has an exception: it does not count NULL values when applied to a specific column, but it does count them when using an asterisk (*).

For example, to count the number of non-NULL 'price' values:

```
SELECT COUNT(price) FROM orders;
```

To count all rows, including those with NULL 'price' values:

```
SELECT COUNT(*) FROM orders;
```

Handling NULL values correctly is crucial for accurate data analysis and reporting. Be sure to practice working with NULL values in your SQL queries to become more proficient in handling missing or unknown data.

Summary

In Chapter 4: Turning Data into Information, we focused on how SQL can extract meaningful information from raw data. We started by discussing the importance of transforming data into information, as this process allows us to derive insights and make informed decisions based on the data. We then provided an overview of key concepts and techniques, such as GROUP BY, HAVING Clause, aggregate functions, calculated fields, aliases, and handling NULL values.

We learned how to use the GROUP BY clause to group data based on one or more columns, enabling us to perform calculations on each group. We also explored the HAVING clause, which works in conjunction with the GROUP BY clause to filter grouped data based on a condition that involves an aggregate function. Next, we delved into aggregate functions (COUNT, SUM, AVG, MIN, and MAX) that allow us to perform calculations on a set of values, returning a single value. We demonstrated how to use these functions in combination with the GROUP BY and HAVING clauses to extract meaningful information from the data.

We then covered calculated fields, which involve creating new columns in a query's result set by performing calculations on existing columns. We demonstrated how to create calculated fields using arithmetic operators and functions, showcasing the power and flexibility of SQL in transforming data. Aliases were introduced as a means to temporarily rename columns or tables in a query, making it more readable and easier to understand. We demonstrated how to use aliases with both columns and tables, showing how they can simplify complex queries or when joining multiple tables. Lastly, we explored handling NULL values, which represent missing or unknown data. We learned how to use the IS NULL and IS NOT NULL operators in the WHERE clause to filter data based on the presence or absence of NULL values. We also discussed the COALESCE() and NULLIF() functions, which provide powerful tools for handling NULL values in queries. Finally, we discussed how aggregate functions handle NULL values, pointing out the exception with the COUNT function.

CHAPTER 5: WORKING WITH TABLES

Creating and Managing Tables

In this chapter, we will explore advanced aspects of creating and managing tables in SQL. We will cover various constraints, data types, and table management techniques that are essential when working with complex tables. We'll use the example.db file as a reference for our examples.

Advanced Data Types

SQLite supports several advanced data types beyond the basic INTEGER, TEXT, and REAL. These data types include BLOB for binary data and NUMERIC for exact numeric values.

For example, to create a table with advanced data types:

```
CREATE TABLE employees (
    employee_id INTEGER PRIMARY KEY,
    first_name TEXT NOT NULL,
    last_name TEXT NOT NULL,
    date_of_birth TEXT,
    salary REAL,
    photo BLOB,
    hire_date NUMERIC
);
```

Constraints

Constraints are rules applied to columns or tables to maintain data integrity and consistency. Common constraints include PRIMARY KEY, FOREIGN KEY, UNIQUE, NOT NULL, and CHECK.

For example, to create a table with various constraints:

```
CREATE TABLE orders (
    order_id INTEGER PRIMARY KEY,
    customer_id INTEGER NOT NULL,
    product_id INTEGER NOT NULL,
    quantity INTEGER CHECK (quantity > 0),
    price REAL,
```

```
  order_date NUMERIC,
  FOREIGN KEY (customer_id) REFERENCES customers(customer_id),
  FOREIGN KEY (product_id) REFERENCES products(product_id),
  UNIQUE (order_id, product_id)
);
```

Indexes

Indexes are database objects that help improve data retrieval performance. Creating an index on one or more columns can speed up the process of searching for specific values.

For example, to create an index on the 'customer_id' column:

```
CREATE INDEX idx_orders_customer_id ON orders(customer_id);
```

ALTER TABLE

The ALTER TABLE statement is used to modify existing tables, such as adding or renaming columns, or changing column data types.

For example, to add a new column 'email' to the 'customers' table:

```
ALTER TABLE customers ADD COLUMN email TEXT;
```

Temporary Tables

Temporary tables are tables that exist only for the duration of a session. They can be useful for storing intermediate results or for breaking down complex queries.

For example, to create a temporary table to store the total sales for each customer:

```
CREATE TEMPORARY TABLE customer_sales AS
SELECT customer_id, SUM(price * quantity) AS total_sales
FROM orders
GROUP BY customer_id;
```

Exploring each of these advanced table management techniques is needed to be equipped to work with complex tables and maintain data integrity and performance in your database.

ALTER TABLE

The ALTER TABLE statement is used to modify the structure of an existing table in a database. With ALTER TABLE, you can add, modify, or drop columns, rename columns, or rename the table itself. This statement is useful when you need to make changes to your table schema without losing the existing data.

ALTER TABLE Operations

Given below are some common ALTER TABLE operations:

Add a new column:

You can add a new column to an existing table using the ADD COLUMN clause.

For example, let us add a new column 'email' to the 'customers' table in the example.db:

```
ALTER TABLE customers ADD COLUMN email TEXT;
```

Rename a column:

You can rename an existing column using the RENAME COLUMN clause.

For example, let us rename the 'email' column to 'contact_email' in the 'customers' table:

```
ALTER TABLE customers RENAME COLUMN email TO contact_email;
```

Modify a column's data type:

You can modify a column's data type using the ALTER COLUMN clause. However, SQLite doesn't support ALTER COLUMN directly. Instead, you need to follow a workaround that involves creating a new table with the desired structure, copying the data, and then renaming the tables.

For example, let us change the data type of the 'contact_email' column from TEXT to VARCHAR(255):

First, create a new table with the desired structure:

```
CREATE TABLE customers_new (
  customer_id INTEGER PRIMARY KEY,
```

```
    first_name TEXT NOT NULL,
    last_name TEXT NOT NULL,
    contact_email VARCHAR(255)
);
```

Next, copy the data from the original 'customers' table to the new table:

```
INSERT INTO customers_new (customer_id, first_name, last_name, contact_email)
SELECT customer_id, first_name, last_name, contact_email
FROM customers;
```

Drop the original table:

```
DROP TABLE customers;
```

Finally, rename the new table to the original table name:

```
ALTER TABLE customers_new RENAME TO customers;
```

Please note that this approach is specific to SQLite. Other databases, like PostgreSQL or MySQL, support modifying a column's data type directly using ALTER TABLE.

Drop a column:

SQLite doesn't support the DROP COLUMN clause directly. Instead, follow the same workaround used for modifying a column's data type: create a new table without the unwanted column, copy the data, and then rename the tables.

For example, let us remove the 'contact_email' column from the 'customers' table:

First, create a new table without the 'contact_email' column:

```
CREATE TABLE customers_new (
    customer_id INTEGER PRIMARY KEY,
    first_name TEXT NOT NULL,
    last_name TEXT NOT NULL
```

```
);
```

Next, copy the data from the original 'customers' table to the new table:

```
INSERT INTO customers_new (customer_id, first_name, last_name)
SELECT customer_id, first_name, last_name
FROM customers;
```

Drop the original table:

```
DROP TABLE customers;
```

Finally, rename the new table to the original table name:

```
ALTER TABLE customers_new RENAME TO customers;
```

Each of these various ALTER TABLE operations makes you confident and skilled to modify existing tables and maintain your database schema effectively.

Primary and Foreign Keys

Primary and foreign keys are essential components of relational databases. They help maintain data integrity and establish relationships between tables.

Primary Key

A primary key is a column (or a combination of columns) that uniquely identifies each row in a table. Each table should have a primary key, and the values in this column must be unique and not null.

In the example.db, the 'customer_id' column in the 'customers' table serves as a primary key:

```
CREATE TABLE customers (
    customer_id INTEGER PRIMARY KEY,
    first_name TEXT NOT NULL,
    last_name TEXT NOT NULL
);
```

Foreign Key

A foreign key is a column (or a combination of columns) in one table that refers to the primary key in another table. It is used to establish a relationship between two tables and enforce referential integrity, which means that if a foreign key value exists in one table, there must be a matching primary key value in the referenced table.

In the example.db, the 'orders' table has a foreign key 'customer_id' that refers to the 'customer_id' primary key in the 'customers' table:

```
CREATE TABLE orders (
    order_id INTEGER PRIMARY KEY,
    customer_id INTEGER NOT NULL,
    product_id INTEGER NOT NULL,
    quantity INTEGER CHECK (quantity > 0),
    price REAL,
    order_date NUMERIC,
    FOREIGN KEY (customer_id) REFERENCES customers(customer_id)
);
```

Working of Primary & Foreign Key

To demonstrate how primary and foreign keys work together, let us insert some data into the 'customers' and 'orders' tables in the example.db:

Insert a new customer:

```
INSERT INTO customers (first_name, last_name)
VALUES ('John', 'Doe');
```

Insert a new order for the customer:

```
INSERT INTO orders (customer_id, product_id, quantity, price, order_date)
VALUES (1, 1, 3, 15.99, '2022-01-01');
```

Since the 'customer_id' in the 'orders' table is a foreign key referring to the 'customers' table, we can't insert an order with a non-existent 'customer_id':

```sql
INSERT INTO orders (customer_id, product_id, quantity, price, order_date)
VALUES (999, 1, 3, 15.99, '2022-01-01');
```

To retrieve data from both tables using primary and foreign keys, we can use JOINs:

```sql
SELECT c.customer_id, c.first_name, c.last_name, o.order_id, o.order_date, o.price
FROM customers c
JOIN orders o ON c.customer_id = o.customer_id;
```

This query will return a result set with customer information along with their orders.

When dealing with relational databases, having a solid understanding of primary and foreign keys, as well as how to use them, is essential since these keys help to ensure data integrity and build associations across tables. When designing your database and running queries, make it a habit to use primary and foreign keys. This will ensure that your data is managed correctly.

Indexes

Indexes are database objects that help improve data retrieval performance. They provide a more efficient way for the database management system (DBMS) to find records when searching for specific values in a table. Indexes are created on one or more columns in a table, and they work similarly to an index in a book, allowing the DBMS to find the desired data quickly without scanning the entire table.

Creating an Index

You can create an index using the CREATE INDEX statement. For example, let's create an index on the 'last_name' column in the 'customers' table in the example.db:

```sql
CREATE INDEX idx_customers_last_name ON customers(last_name);
```

This index will make searches based on the 'last_name' column faster. However, it's essential to note that indexes come with some trade-offs. While they can speed up data retrieval, they can also slow down data modification operations (INSERT, UPDATE, DELETE) because the index must be updated whenever the table data changes. So, it's crucial to create indexes only on columns that are frequently used in WHERE clauses or JOIN conditions.

Using an Index

The database management system automatically utilizes indexes when executing queries, so you don't need to change your SQL queries to take advantage of them. The DBMS optimizer will choose the most efficient index to use based on the query conditions. For example, when querying customers by their last name, the DBMS will use the 'idx_customers_last_name' index to speed up the search:

```
SELECT * FROM customers WHERE last_name = 'Smith';
```

Dropping an Index

If you find that an index is no longer needed or negatively impacting performance, you can drop it using the DROP INDEX statement. For example, to drop the 'idx_customers_last_name' index:

```
DROP INDEX idx_customers_last_name;
```

Remember that dropping an index can cause query performance to degrade if the index was being used by the DBMS to optimize searches.

In a nutshell, indexes are an indispensable component of effective database optimization. They have the potential to dramatically increase the performance of data retrieval when applied correctly. However, they come with drawbacks, therefore it is essential to carefully assess whether and when to employ them before committing to their implementation. You can improve the performance of your database and write SQL queries that are more effective if you have a solid understanding of how indexes function and make strategic use of them.

Dropping Tables

Dropping tables is an essential operation in database management when it becomes necessary to permanently eliminate a specific table from your database. This action not only removes the table structure itself, but also eradicates all the data that has been stored within the table. Additionally, any related constraints, triggers, or indexes that are associated with the table in question will also be deleted. This process is critical when restructuring databases, maintaining data integrity, or simply removing outdated or unnecessary information from the system.

To drop a table in SQLite, you use the DROP TABLE statement followed by the table name you want to remove.

For example, let's assume we have a table named 'temp_data' in the example.db that we no longer need. To drop this table, you would execute the following SQL statement:

```
DROP TABLE temp_data;
```

Please note that dropping a table is irreversible, and you will lose all the data stored in the table. Therefore, it's crucial to ensure that you have a backup of the data if you might need it in the future or to double-check your decision before executing the DROP TABLE statement.

When you drop a table that has foreign key relationships with other tables, you must handle these relationships appropriately. If a table you're dropping has foreign keys referencing it in other tables, you should either:

1. Remove the foreign key constraints from the referencing tables before dropping the table.
2. Drop the referencing tables before dropping the referenced table.

For example, let us assume that we have a 'products' table in example.db, and the 'orders' table has a foreign key 'product_id' that refers to the 'product_id' primary key in the 'products' table. If you want to drop the 'products' table, you must first either drop the 'orders' table or remove the foreign key constraint in the 'orders' table. Otherwise, you'll encounter an error due to the existing foreign key relationship.

To summarize, dropping tables is an operation that must be performed when maintaining databases. However, because executing the DROP TABLE statement permanently deletes both the table and its contents, it is vitally crucial to exercise extreme caution whenever doing so. Before you ever drop a table, you must ensure that you have a backup of your data and that any foreign key relationships are appropriately handled.

Constraints

Constraints are essential rules applied to table columns in a database management system to guarantee that the data stored within the table complies with specific requirements or conditions. These constraints play a crucial role in preserving data integrity, consistency, and accuracy across the entire database. By enforcing these rules, constraints help prevent the entry of incorrect or inconsistent data, ensuring that the information is reliable, easy to query, and in line with the predefined standards set by the database designer or administrator.

Some common types of constraints include:

PRIMARY KEY

This constraint ensures that each row in the table has a unique identifier. A primary key column cannot have NULL values, and each value must be unique. A table can have only one primary key, but it can consist of multiple columns (composite primary key).

Example:

```
CREATE TABLE customers (
  customer_id INTEGER PRIMARY KEY,
  first_name TEXT,
  last_name TEXT
);
```

FOREIGN KEY

This constraint is used to establish a relationship between two tables. A foreign key in one table refers to the primary key of another table, ensuring that the data in the foreign key column(s) exists in the referenced primary key column(s).

Example:

```
CREATE TABLE orders (
  order_id INTEGER PRIMARY KEY,
  customer_id INTEGER,
  order_date TEXT,
  FOREIGN KEY (customer_id) REFERENCES customers (customer_id)
);
```

UNIQUE

This constraint ensures that all values in a column are unique. Unlike primary keys, UNIQUE columns can have NULL values, but each non-NULL value must be unique.

Example:

```
CREATE TABLE employees (
  employee_id INTEGER PRIMARY KEY,
```

email TEXT UNIQUE,
  first_name TEXT,
  last_name TEXT
);
```

## CHECK

The CHECK constraint is used to ensure that the data in a column meets a specific condition. The condition can be any valid SQL expression that evaluates to a boolean result (TRUE or FALSE).

Example:

```
CREATE TABLE products (
  product_id INTEGER PRIMARY KEY,
  name TEXT,
  price REAL CHECK (price >= 0)
);
```

NOT NULL

This constraint enforces that a column cannot contain NULL values. Every row in the table must have a value for that column. The NOT NULL constraint is often used in conjunction with PRIMARY KEY constraints, as primary keys cannot have NULL values.

Example:

```
CREATE TABLE students (
  student_id INTEGER PRIMARY KEY,
  first_name TEXT NOT NULL,
  last_name TEXT NOT NULL,
  age INTEGER
);
```
```

DEFAULT

The DEFAULT constraint is used to provide a default value for a column when a new row is inserted. If no value is provided for that column during an INSERT operation, the default value will be used automatically.

Example:

```
CREATE TABLE tasks (
  task_id INTEGER PRIMARY KEY,
  description TEXT NOT NULL,
  status TEXT DEFAULT 'pending'
);
```

When creating tables, it's essential to define appropriate constraints to maintain data integrity and consistency within the database. Constraints help ensure that the data stored in the table adheres to specific requirements or conditions, preventing the insertion of invalid or inconsistent data. You may construct a robust and reliable database schema that enforces data validation rules and boosts overall database performance by carefully specifying and utilizing constraints. This allows you to create a robust and reliable database.

Summary

In Chapter 5, we delved into the more complex aspects of working with tables in SQL. We began by learning how to create complex tables and discussing the different column data types and their applications. Using example.db as a reference, we also explored how to design and create tables with multiple columns and relationships.

Next, we explored the ALTER TABLE statement, a powerful tool for modifying existing table structures. We learned how to add new columns, change column data types, and rename columns, all without affecting the data stored in the table. This flexibility allows database designers to adapt and evolve their schema as requirements change over time. We then discussed the concept of primary and foreign keys, which are essential for establishing relationships between tables and maintaining referential integrity. By using primary and foreign keys, we can create a robust and interconnected database schema that ensures data consistency and prevents the insertion of invalid data.

Following that, we investigated indexes, which are database objects that improve data retrieval performance. By creating indexes on specific columns, we can significantly speed up search operations and improve overall database efficiency. We also learned how to drop tables, a crucial operation when removing unwanted or obsolete tables from a database. Dropping tables permanently deletes the table structure, data, and associated objects such as constraints, triggers, and indexes. We discussed the importance of handling foreign key relationships and backing up data before executing DROP TABLE statements. Lastly, we examined various types of constraints that help maintain data integrity and consistency within the database. We discussed PRIMARY KEY, FOREIGN KEY, UNIQUE, CHECK, NOT NULL, and DEFAULT constraints, and demonstrated how they can be used to enforce specific requirements or conditions on table columns.

Chapter 6: Multiple Tables and Joins

Overview

In this chapter, we focus on working with multiple tables and joins, which are essential concepts in relational databases. When designing a database, it's common to break down the data into multiple related tables to maintain a well-structured and organized schema. This process is known as normalization, and it helps reduce data redundancy and improve data integrity.

The need for multiple tables arises from the requirement to store complex data and relationships. In real-world scenarios, data is often interconnected, and representing these connections in a single table can lead to inefficiencies and redundancies. By dividing the data into multiple related tables, we can achieve better organization, flexibility, and performance.

Joins come into play when we need to retrieve data from multiple related tables. In SQL, joins are used to combine data from two or more tables based on a related column, usually a foreign key. Joins enable us to merge and filter data from different tables to create a meaningful result set, providing a powerful way to query and analyze data.

In this chapter, we will explore table relationships and different types of joins, understand their use cases, and learn how to implement them in SQL queries. By mastering multiple tables and joins, you will be able to handle complex data relationships and extract valuable insights from your database.

Table Relationships

Table relationships form the basis of relational databases, providing a structure to represent the connections between various entities within the database. By establishing these relationships, users can efficiently manage, retrieve, and analyze data. There are three primary types of relationships that help maintain data integrity and ensure the accuracy of information:

One-to-One (1:1)

In a one-to-one relationship, one record in a table is related to exactly one record in another table. This type of relationship is less common in practice but can be useful in specific scenarios.

Example: Suppose we have two tables, employees and employee_details. Each employee has a unique set of personal details. Here, each record in the employees table is related to exactly one record in the employee_details table.

```sql
CREATE TABLE employees (
  id INTEGER PRIMARY KEY,
  first_name TEXT NOT NULL,
  last_name TEXT NOT NULL
);
```

```sql
CREATE TABLE employee_details (
  id INTEGER PRIMARY KEY,
  employee_id INTEGER UNIQUE REFERENCES employees(id),
  phone_number TEXT,
  address TEXT
);
```

One-to-Many (1:N)

In a one-to-many relationship, one record in a table can be related to multiple records in another table, but each record in the other table is related to only one record in the first table.

Example: Consider the tables authors and books. One author can write multiple books, but each book has only one author. Here, one record in the authors table is related to multiple records in the books table.

```sql
CREATE TABLE authors (
  id INTEGER PRIMARY KEY,
  name TEXT NOT NULL
);
```

```sql
CREATE TABLE books (
  id INTEGER PRIMARY KEY,
  title TEXT NOT NULL,
  author_id INTEGER REFERENCES authors(id)
);
```

<u>Many-to-Many (M:N)</u>

In a many-to-many relationship, one record in a table can be related to multiple records in another table, and vice versa. This type of relationship is often represented using a junction table or associative entity, which holds foreign keys of both related tables.

Example: Take the tables students and courses. A student can enroll in multiple courses, and a course can have multiple students. Here, records in the students table are related to records in the courses table through the student_courses junction table.

```
CREATE TABLE students (
  id INTEGER PRIMARY KEY,
  name TEXT NOT NULL
);
```

```
CREATE TABLE courses (
  id INTEGER PRIMARY KEY,
  name TEXT NOT NULL
);
```

```
CREATE TABLE student_courses (
  student_id INTEGER REFERENCES students(id),
  course_id INTEGER REFERENCES courses(id),
  PRIMARY KEY (student_id, course_id)
);
```

Understanding table relationships and their importance in SQL is crucial for designing a well-structured database schema and efficiently querying related data using joins. By effectively representing real-world relationships between entities, you can create a flexible and robust database that accurately reflects the complexity of the underlying data.

INNER JOIN

INNER JOIN is the most common type of join in SQL. It returns only the rows where there is a match in both tables based on the specified condition. In other words, an INNER JOIN retrieves records from both tables where there is a match between the values in the related columns.

Let us understand INNER JOIN with a demonstration using the example.db. Consider the following two tables, authors and books:

```sql
CREATE TABLE authors (
  id INTEGER PRIMARY KEY,
  name TEXT NOT NULL
);
```

```sql
CREATE TABLE books (
  id INTEGER PRIMARY KEY,
  title TEXT NOT NULL,
  author_id INTEGER REFERENCES authors(id)
);
```

Suppose we want to get a list of all books along with their respective authors. We can use INNER JOIN to combine the authors and books tables based on the author_id foreign key in the books table:

```sql
SELECT authors.name AS author_name, books.title AS book_title
FROM authors
INNER JOIN books ON authors.id = books.author_id;
```

In this query, we use the INNER JOIN keyword followed by the table we want to join (books). The ON keyword is used to specify the condition for the join: authors.id = books.author_id. This condition matches the id column in the authors table with the author_id column in the books table.

The query returns a result set with the columns author_name and book_title, which represent the names of the authors and the titles of their respective books. Only rows with a match in both tables, i.e., rows where the author_id in the books table matches the id in the authors table, will be included in the result set.

We are able to retrieve related data from various tables in an effective manner thanks to the INNER JOIN function, which in turn enables us to analyze and present the data in a manner that is more meaningful to the user.

OUTER JOIN

Now let us explore other types of joins in SQL, starting with OUTER JOINs.

OUTER JOINs can be further categorized into LEFT OUTER JOIN (or simply LEFT JOIN), RIGHT OUTER JOIN (or RIGHT JOIN), and FULL OUTER JOIN (or FULL JOIN). These joins return not only the matching rows from both tables but also the unmatched rows from one or both tables, depending on the type of OUTER JOIN used.

LEFT JOIN (LEFT OUTER JOIN)

The LEFT JOIN returns all rows from the left table (table specified before the JOIN keyword) and the matched rows from the right table (table specified after the JOIN keyword). If there is no match, NULL values are returned for columns from the right table.

Let us demonstrate LEFT JOIN using the authors and books tables in example.db. Suppose we want to get a list of all authors along with their books, including authors who haven't written any books:

```
SELECT authors.name AS author_name, books.title AS book_title
FROM authors
LEFT JOIN books ON authors.id = books.author_id;
```

In this query, we use the LEFT JOIN keyword instead of INNER JOIN. The result set will include all rows from the authors table, and if there is no match in the books table (i.e., the author has not written any books), NULL values will be displayed for the book_title column.

RIGHT JOIN (RIGHT OUTER JOIN)

The RIGHT JOIN works similarly to the LEFT JOIN, but it returns all rows from the right table and the matched rows from the left table. If there is no match, NULL values are returned for columns from the left table.

Since SQLite does not support RIGHT JOIN directly, you can achieve the same result by reversing the order of the tables and using a LEFT JOIN. Let us assume we have two tables authors and books, and we want to list all books and their authors, including the books that have no authors.

Below is how you would do it using a RIGHT JOIN equivalent in SQLite:

```sql
SELECT authors.name AS author_name, books.title AS book_title
FROM books
LEFT JOIN authors ON authors.id = books.author_id;
```

By reversing the order of the tables and using a LEFT JOIN, you get the same result as a RIGHT JOIN would provide.

FULL JOIN (FULL OUTER JOIN)

The FULL JOIN returns all rows when there is a match in either the left or right table. If there is no match, NULL values are returned for the columns of the table with no match. SQLite does not support FULL JOIN directly, but you can achieve the same result using a combination of LEFT JOIN and UNION.

To demonstrate this, let us assume we have two tables employees and departments, and we want to list all employees and their departments, including employees without departments and departments without employees.

Below is how you would do it using a FULL JOIN equivalent in SQLite:

```sql
-- Left Join
SELECT employees.name AS employee_name, departments.name AS
department_name
FROM employees
LEFT JOIN departments ON employees.department_id = departments.id
```

```sql
-- Right Join equivalent (using Left Join)
SELECT employees.name AS employee_name, departments.name AS
department_name
FROM departments
LEFT JOIN employees ON employees.department_id = departments.id
WHERE employees.id IS NULL;
```

In this query, we first perform a LEFT JOIN to get all employees and their departments, including employees without departments. Then, we use a UNION to combine the results of the LEFT JOIN with the results of a RIGHT JOIN equivalent (achieved by reversing the order of the tables and using a LEFT JOIN) to get all departments without employees. The final result is the same as a FULL JOIN.

OUTER JOINs allow you to retrieve not only the matching rows from both tables, but also the mismatched rows from one or both tables, depending on the type of OUTER JOIN utilized. If you wish to do an analysis in which you include all records from one or both tables, regardless of whether or not there is a match in the linked column(s), this can be a good technique to employ.

CROSS JOIN

The last type of join we'll discuss is the CROSS JOIN. A CROSS JOIN, also known as a Cartesian join, returns the Cartesian product of the two tables involved in the join. In other words, it returns all possible combinations of rows from the left table with rows from the right table. Unlike INNER JOIN and OUTER JOIN, CROSS JOIN does not require a join condition.

Let us demonstrate a CROSS JOIN using the authors and books tables in example.db. Suppose we want to see all possible combinations of authors and book titles:

```
SELECT authors.name AS author_name, books.title AS book_title
FROM authors
CROSS JOIN books;
```

In this query, we use the CROSS JOIN keyword to combine the authors and books tables. The result set will contain all possible combinations of author names and book titles, even if the authors did not write those specific books.

It's essential to note that CROSS JOINs can produce a large number of rows, especially if the tables involved have many records. Therefore, use CROSS JOINs cautiously and consider if there are more appropriate join types to use for your specific situation.

Just to sum it up, SQL provides several types of JOINs—INNER JOIN, OUTER JOIN (LEFT, RIGHT, and FULL), and CROSS JOIN—to combine data from multiple tables. Each join type has its specific use cases, depending on the relationship between the tables and the desired output. Understanding these join types and their applications is crucial for a SQL developer to efficiently retrieve and analyze data from multiple tables in a relational database.

UNION and UNION ALL

UNION is an SQL operation used to combine the result sets of two or more SELECT queries into a single result set. The UNION operator removes duplicate rows from the combined result set. To use UNION, the SELECT queries involved must have the same number of columns, and the corresponding columns must have compatible data types.

Let us consider an example using the authors and books tables in example.db. Suppose we want to create a list of all author names and book titles in a single column. We can use the UNION operator to achieve this:

```sql
SELECT authors.name AS name
FROM authors

UNION

SELECT books.title AS name
FROM books;
```

In this query, we first select all author names from the authors table, and then we use the UNION operator to combine these results with the book titles from the books table. The result set will include all unique author names and book titles in a single column named name.

If you want to include all rows from both SELECT queries, including duplicates, you can use the UNION ALL operator instead:

```sql
SELECT authors.name AS name
FROM authors

UNION ALL

SELECT books.title AS name
FROM books;
```

The UNION ALL operator combines the result sets from both SELECT queries without removing duplicates.

The UNION and UNION ALL operators allow you to combine the result sets of two or more SELECT queries into a single result set. This can be useful when you need to retrieve and analyze data from different tables with a similar structure, or when you want to merge data from multiple sources in a single query.

Normalization and Denormalization

Normalization and denormalization are two database design concepts that deal with the organization and optimization of data in a relational database.

Objective of Normalization

Normalization is the process of organizing data in a database to reduce data redundancy and improve data integrity. It involves decomposing a table into smaller, more manageable tables and defining relationships between them. Normalization is based on a set of rules, called normal forms, that directs the design of a well-structured and efficient database.

The primary goals of normalization are:
- Eliminate redundant data: By organizing data into smaller tables and linking them through relationships, normalization helps remove data redundancy, making the database more efficient and easier to maintain.
- Ensure data integrity: By minimizing redundancy, normalization also helps maintain data integrity, as it becomes less likely that data inconsistencies will occur when inserting, updating, or deleting records.
- Optimize the database structure: Normalized databases are usually better optimized for query performance, as smaller tables with fewer columns are faster to read and require less memory.

Objective of Denormalization

Denormalization is the process of adding redundant data back into the database to improve query performance. It is the opposite of normalization and is often used when read performance is more critical than write performance or when database size is not a concern.

The primary goal of denormalization is to:
- Improve query performance: By adding redundant data or precomputed values to the database, denormalization can reduce the number of joins and aggregations needed to answer a query, leading to faster query execution times.

However, denormalization comes with its drawbacks:
- Increased data redundancy: By design, denormalization introduces redundancy, making the database larger and more complex to maintain.

- Reduced data integrity: With redundant data, the risk of data inconsistencies increases when inserting, updating, or deleting records.

Database designers must strike a balance between normalization and denormalization, considering factors such as performance requirements, data integrity, and maintenance complexity. It is essential to understand these concepts and their trade-offs to make informed decisions when designing and optimizing a relational database.

Applying Normalization

To understand and practice normalization, let us go through the step-by-step process using the first three normal forms (1NF, 2NF, and 3NF). These are the most commonly used normal forms in database design.

We will use a hypothetical table with some data as an example, and then you can apply the same principles to the example.db.

Suppose you have the following table named orders:

OrderID	CustomerName	Product Name	Quantity	Price	OrderDate
1	John Smith	Laptop	1	1000	2022-01-01
2	Jane Doe	Monitor	2	150	2022-01-02
3	John Smith	Keyboard	1	30	2022-01-03

First Normal Form (1NF)

To achieve 1NF, we need to ensure that each column contains only atomic values (single, indivisible values) and that there are no repeating groups of columns. Our above example table is already in 1NF, so no changes are needed.

Second Normal Form (2NF)

To achieve 2NF, we need to make sure that all non-key columns are fully dependent on the primary key. In other words, there should be no partial dependencies.

Looking at the orders table, we can see that the CustomerName and ProductName columns are not fully dependent on the OrderID. To fix this, we can create separate tables for customers, products, and orders.

Customers table:

CustomerID	CustomerName
1	John Smith
2	Jane Doe

Products table:

ProductID	ProductName	Price
1	Laptop	1000
2	Monitor	150
3	Keyboard	30

Orders table:

OrderID	CustomerID	ProductID	Quantity	OrderDate
1	1	1	1	2022-01-01
2	2	2	2	2022-01-02
3	1	3	1	2022-01-03

Now the orders table is in 2NF.

Third Normal Form (3NF)

To achieve 3NF, we need to ensure that all non-key columns are directly dependent on the primary key and not on other non-key columns. In other words, there should be no transitive dependencies.

Looking at the products table, we can see that the Price column is dependent on the ProductName. To fix this, we can create separate tables for products and prices.

product_prices table:

PriceID	ProductID	Price
1	1	1000
2	2	150
3	3	30

Now our database is in 3NF.

To practice normalization on the example.db, you can follow the same steps and identify the dependencies and redundancies in your tables.

Applying Denormalization

Denormalization is the process of adding redundant data or combining tables to improve the read performance of a database. While normalization aims to eliminate redundancy and improve the structure, denormalization intentionally introduces redundancy for performance gains.

The key to denormalization is to strike a balance between query performance and data integrity. The given below is an easy technique for denormalization using a simple example.

Consider that we have three normalized tables in 3NF:

Customers table:

CustomerID	CustomerName
1	John Smith
2	Jane Doe

Products table:

ProductID	ProductName
1	Laptop
2	Monitor
3	Keyboard

Orders table:

OrderID	CustomerID	ProductID	Quantity	OrderDate
1	1	1	1	2022-01-01
2	2	2	2	2022-01-02
3	1	3	1	2022-01-03

Now, suppose we want to denormalize the data to reduce the number of JOINs required to retrieve order information, which will improve the read performance.

To achieve this, we can create a new table called orders_denormalized that combines data from the customers, products, and orders tables:

Orders_denormalized table:

OrderID	CustomerID	CustomerName	ProductID	ProductName	Quantity	OrderDate
1	1	John Smith	1	Laptop	1	2022-01-01
2	2	Jane Doe	2	Monitor	2	2022-01-02
3	1	John Smith	3	Keyboard	1	2022-01-03

By doing this, we have introduced redundancy to our database but reduced the need for JOINs when querying order information. This can lead to faster read performance at the cost of increased storage and more complex updates.

When you're denormalizing your example.db, identify the most common or performance-critical queries and decide which tables can be combined to improve read performance. Keep in mind that denormalization can lead to data anomalies and inconsistencies if not managed carefully, so always weigh the benefits against the potential drawbacks. A proper denormalization strategy considers both the advantages and potential downsides. Always monitor the performance and data integrity of your denormalized database to ensure it meets your requirements.

Summary

In this Chapter, we delved into the world of multiple tables and joins. We started with understanding the necessity of multiple tables and the concept of table relationships. We learned that tables can be related to each other through primary and foreign keys, and that there are different types of relationships, such as one-to-one, one-to-many, and many-to-many.

Next, we explored JOINs in detail, focusing on INNER JOIN, LEFT JOIN, and CROSS JOIN. We learned that INNER JOIN returns only the rows with matching values in both tables, LEFT JOIN returns all rows from the left table and matching rows from the right table, and CROSS JOIN returns the Cartesian product of rows from the tables. We also discussed how to achieve RIGHT JOIN and FULL JOIN in SQLite using LEFT JOIN and UNION. We then proceeded to understand the UNION operator, which is used to combine the result sets of two or more SELECT statements. We learned that UNION removes duplicate rows and returns the combined result set in ascending order, while UNION ALL retains duplicates and does not sort the results.

Normalization and denormalization were also covered in this chapter. We learned that normalization is the process of organizing data in a database to reduce redundancy and improve data integrity. We explored the various normal forms, such as 1NF, 2NF, and 3NF, and discussed an easy technique for normalizing a database. Denormalization, on the other hand, is the process of adding redundant data or combining tables to improve read performance. We learned an easy technique for denormalization and discussed the potential benefits and drawbacks of denormalizing a database.

Chapter 7: SQL Functions

Built-in Functions Overview

In this chapter, we will explore SQL functions, which are pre-defined procedures used to manipulate and process data in a database. Functions enable developers to perform calculations, format data, and simplify complex query logic, thus enhancing the capabilities of SQL queries.

There are several categories of SQL functions, each serving a specific purpose:

Built-in functions: These are standard functions provided by the database management system. They can be broadly classified into the following types:

- String functions: These functions are used to manipulate, compare, and analyze character and string data. Examples include LENGTH, CONCAT, SUBSTR, and REPLACE.
- Date and time functions: These functions are used to work with date and time data types, such as extracting specific components (year, month, day, etc.), adding or subtracting intervals, and formatting dates. Examples include DATE, TIME, NOW, DATEDIFF, and DATE_FORMAT.
- Numeric functions: These functions are used to perform calculations and operations on numeric data. Examples include ABS, ROUND, CEIL, FLOOR, and MOD.
- Conditional functions: These functions are used to perform conditional operations, such as evaluating expressions based on specific conditions. Examples include IF, CASE, COALESCE, and NULLIF.

Aggregate functions: These functions are used to perform calculations on a set of values and return a single value. They are commonly used in conjunction with the GROUP BY clause. Examples include COUNT, SUM, AVG, MIN, and MAX.

Window functions: These functions are used to perform calculations across a set of rows related to the current row, enabling complex analysis and reporting. Examples include ROW_NUMBER, RANK, DENSE_RANK, NTILE, and CUME_DIST.

User-defined functions: These are custom functions created by developers to encapsulate specific business logic or perform unique calculations that are not available through built-in functions. User-defined functions help to improve code reusability and maintainability.

In the following sections of this chapter, we will go deeper into each type of functions, and we will learn how to utilize them successfully by utilizing the example.db to walk through some practical instances of their use. You will be able to manage and analyze data in a way that is more efficient and accurate once you have completed this chapter because you will have a thorough understanding of SQL functions and their applications.

String Functions

String functions play a vital role in managing, comparing, and examining character and string data within SQL queries. They are indispensable tools for handling text data efficiently and accurately when working with databases. In this article, we will explore several commonly used string functions and illustrate their practical applications with examples using the example.db database.

LENGTH(str)

Returns the length of the input string 'str'.

Example:

```
SELECT LENGTH(name) AS name_length FROM employees;
```

This query returns the length of the 'name' column for each record in the 'employees' table.

CONCAT(str1, str2, ...)

Concatenates two or more strings.

Example:

```
SELECT CONCAT(first_name, ' ', last_name) AS full_name FROM employees;
```

This query concatenates the 'first_name' and 'last_name' columns to create a single 'full_name' column for each employee.

SUBSTR(str, start, length)

Extracts a substring from the input string 'str', beginning at the 'start' position and continuing for 'length' characters.

Example:

```
SELECT SUBSTR(name, 1, 3) AS name_short FROM employees;
```

This query extracts the first three characters from the 'name' column for each record in the 'employees' table.

REPLACE(str, from_str, to_str)

Replaces all occurrences of the substring 'from_str' in the input string 'str' with the substring 'to_str'.

Example:

```
SELECT REPLACE(email, '@example.com', '@newdomain.com') AS
updated_email FROM employees;
```

This query replaces the domain '@example.com' with '@newdomain.com' in the 'email' column for each record in the 'employees' table.

UPPER(str) and LOWER(str)

Convert the input string 'str' to uppercase and lowercase, respectively.

Example:

```
SELECT UPPER(name) AS name_upper, LOWER(name) AS name_lower FROM
employees;
```

This query returns the 'name' column in uppercase and lowercase for each record in the 'employees' table.

TRIM(str)

Removes leading and trailing spaces from the input string 'str'.

Example:

```
SELECT TRIM(name) AS trimmed_name FROM employees;
```

This query removes any leading and trailing spaces from the 'name' column for each record in the 'employees' table.

LTRIM(str) and RTRIM(str)

Remove leading spaces (LTRIM) or trailing spaces (RTRIM) from the input string 'str'.

Example:

SELECT LTRIM(name) AS left_trimmed, RTRIM(name) AS right_trimmed FROM employees;

This query removes leading spaces from the 'name' column (left_trimmed) and trailing spaces (right_trimmed) for each record in the 'employees' table.

POSITION(substr IN str)

Returns the position of the first occurrence of the substring 'substr' in the input string 'str'. Returns 0 if the substring is not found.

Example:

SELECT POSITION('@' IN email) AS at_position FROM employees;

This query returns the position of the '@' character in the 'email' column for each record in the 'employees' table.

CHAR_LENGTH(str)

Returns the number of characters in the input string 'str'. This function is similar to LENGTH, but it considers multi-byte characters as a single character.

Example:

SELECT CHAR_LENGTH(name) AS char_length FROM employees;

This query returns the number of characters in the 'name' column for each record in the 'employees' table, taking into account multi-byte characters.

REVERSE(str)

Reverses the characters in the input string 'str'.

Example:

SELECT REVERSE(name) AS reversed_name FROM employees;

This query returns the 'name' column with its characters reversed for each record in the 'employees' table.

These are just a few examples of string functions that can be used to modify and analyze text data within SQL. There are many more. You are able to conduct a variety of actions on strings by making use of these methods, such as concatenating, extracting, replacing, and altering the case of individual letters. When you're dealing with text data, adding string functions to your SQL toolset is an excellent decision because they can considerably boost the adaptability and effectiveness of your queries.

Date and Time Functions

Date and time functions play a crucial role in SQL, allowing you to perform operations on date and time values, extract specific date parts, and perform calculations with date and time data.

Given below are some essential date and time functions in SQL and how to use them with the example.db:

CURRENT_DATE

Returns the current date.

Example:

```
SELECT CURRENT_DATE AS today;
```

This query returns the current date.

CURRENT_TIME

Returns the current time.

Example:

```
SELECT CURRENT_TIME AS now;
```

This query returns the current time.

DATE_PART(part, date)

Extracts a specific part of a date value ('year', 'month', 'day', 'hour', 'minute', 'second').
Example:

```
SELECT DATE_PART('year', hire_date) AS hire_year FROM employees;
```

This query extracts the 'year' part from the 'hire_date' column for each record in the 'employees' table.

DATE_TRUNC(unit, date)

Truncates the date value to a specified unit ('year', 'quarter', 'month', 'week', 'day', 'hour', 'minute', 'second').

Example:

```
SELECT DATE_TRUNC('month', hire_date) AS month_start FROM employees;
```

This query truncates the 'hire_date' column to the start of the month for each record in the 'employees' table.

AGE(timestamp)

Calculates the age between the specified timestamp and the current date.

Example:

```
SELECT AGE(hire_date) AS tenure FROM employees;
```

This query calculates the tenure of each employee based on their 'hire_date' in the 'employees' table.

EXTRACT(part FROM date)

Extracts a specific part of a date value (similar to DATE_PART).

Example:

```
SELECT EXTRACT(year FROM hire_date) AS hire_year FROM employees;
```

This query extracts the 'year' part from the 'hire_date' column for each record in the 'employees' table.

INTERVAL

Used to perform arithmetic with date and time values.

Example:

```
SELECT hire_date + INTERVAL '1 month' AS next_month FROM employees;
```

This query calculates the date one month after the 'hire_date' for each record in the 'employees' table.

When dealing with date and time data in SQL, these date and time functions, which have been introduced above, are indispensable tools. You will be able to rapidly process and modify date and time values, do computations, and extract specific date sections if you learn and master these functions. This will allow you to acquire useful insights from your data.

Numeric Functions

Numeric functions in SQL are used for performing mathematical operations and calculations on numeric data. They are essential tools when working with numeric data types, such as integers and decimals.

Given below are some common numeric functions and how to use them with the example.db:

ABS(x)

Returns the absolute value of a number.

Example:

```
SELECT ABS(-5) AS absolute_value;
```

This query returns the absolute value of -5, which is 5.

ROUND(x, n)

Rounds a number to the specified number of decimal places.

Example:

SELECT ROUND(3.14159, 2) AS rounded_value;

This query rounds the value 3.14159 to two decimal places, resulting in 3.14.

FLOOR(x)

Returns the largest integer value less than or equal to x.

Example:

SELECT FLOOR(3.9) AS floor_value;

This query returns the floor value of 3.9, which is 3.

CEIL(x) or CEILING(x)

Returns the smallest integer value greater than or equal to x.

Example:

SELECT CEILING(3.1) AS ceiling_value;

This query returns the ceiling value of 3.1, which is 4.

POWER(x, y)

Raises x to the power of y.

Example:

SELECT POWER(2, 3) AS power_value;

This query calculates 2 raised to the power of 3, which is 8.

SQRT(x)

Returns the square root of x.

Example:

SELECT SQRT(9) AS square_root;

This query calculates the square root of 9, which is 3.

MOD(x, y)

Returns the remainder of x divided by y.

Example:

SELECT MOD(10, 3) AS modulus;

This query calculates the remainder of 10 divided by 3, which is 1.

RAND()

Generates a random decimal number between 0 and 1.

Example:

SELECT RAND() AS random_number;

This query generates a random decimal number between 0 and 1.

SQL users have access to strong tools that may be used to do mathematical operations and computations thanks to the numeric functions. You will be able to efficiently process and manipulate numeric data, do computations, and produce random numbers if you learn and master these functions, which will enable you to acquire useful insights from your data.

Conditional Functions

Conditional functions in SQL allow you to perform different actions based on specific conditions or criteria. They can help you manage complex data processing, return values based on conditions, or perform calculations using conditional logic.

Given below are some common conditional functions and how to use them with the example.db:

CASE Expression

The CASE expression allows you to perform conditional logic in SQL queries by returning a value based on a condition or set of conditions.

Example:

```sql
SELECT name, salary,
    CASE
        WHEN salary < 30000 THEN 'Low'
        WHEN salary >= 30000 AND salary < 50000 THEN 'Medium'
        ELSE 'High'
    END AS salary_range
FROM employees;
```

This query assigns a salary range ('Low', 'Medium', or 'High') based on the employee's salary.

COALESCE(x1, x2, ..., xn)

The COALESCE function returns the first non-NULL value in a list of expressions.

Example:

```sql
SELECT COALESCE(NULL, 'Hello', 'World') AS first_non_null_value;
```

This query returns the first non-NULL value in the list, which is 'Hello'.

NULLIF(x, y)

The NULLIF function compares two expressions and returns NULL if they are equal, or the first expression if they are not equal.

Example:

```sql
SELECT NULLIF(5, 5) AS null_if_equal;
```

This query returns NULL since the two expressions are equal.

<u>IIF(condition, true_value, false_value)</u>

The IIF function is a shorthand way of writing a simple CASE expression. It returns the true_value if the condition is true, and the false_value if the condition is false.

Example:

```
SELECT IIF(salary > 50000, 'High', 'Low') AS salary_category
FROM employees;
```

This query returns 'High' for employees with a salary greater than 50,000 and 'Low' for others.

You may do more complex data manipulation and return values based on specific conditions if you understand and use the conditional functions in SQL. These functions can help you create queries that are more efficient and flexible if you understand and use them.

Creating User-defined Functions (UDFs)

SQLite allows you to create user-defined functions (UDFs) to extend its functionality. UDFs can be written in various programming languages, such as Python or C, and then loaded into SQLite. Below is a sample program of how to create a UDF using Python and the sqlite3 module:

First, make sure you have Python and the sqlite3 module installed on your system. The sqlite3 module comes pre-installed with Python 2.5+ and 3.x.

Create a new Python file (e.g., my_udf.py) and import the sqlite3 module:

```
import sqlite3
```

Define your UDF. In the below example, we'll create a simple function to calculate the square of a number:

```
def square(x):
    return x * x
```

Connect to the example.db database using the sqlite3.connect() method:

```
conn = sqlite3.connect('example.db')
```

Register your UDF using the create_function() method of the connection object:

```
conn.create_function('square', 1, square)
```

The first argument is the name of the function as it will be used in SQL queries. The second argument is the number of arguments the function takes, and the third argument is the function itself.

Now you can use the square function in your SQL queries:

```
cursor = conn.cursor()
cursor.execute('SELECT square(salary) FROM employees;')
result = cursor.fetchall()
print(result)
```

Close the connection to the database:

```
conn.close()
```

By creating user-defined functions, you can extend the functionality of SQLite and tailor it to your specific needs. Whether you need to perform complex calculations or apply custom business logic, UDFs offer a flexible way to enhance your SQL queries and make them more powerful and efficient.

SQL Functions Best Practices

After learning about creating user-defined functions, let us now discuss some best practices and tips when working with SQL functions:

1. Use built-in functions whenever possible: Built-in functions are usually faster and more efficient than user-defined functions. Always check if there's a built-in function that can perform the required operation before creating a custom function.

2. Keep functions simple and focused: Do not forget that each function has a single responsibility and performs one specific task. This makes your functions easier to

maintain and debug.

3. Use meaningful function names: Choose descriptive names for your functions that clearly indicate their purpose. This makes your SQL queries more readable and easier to understand.

4. Optimize function performance: Ensure your functions are optimized for performance by using efficient algorithms and minimizing resource usage. Avoid using loops and recursion whenever possible, as they can slow down the execution of your functions.

5. Test your functions thoroughly: Do not forget to test your functions with various input values to ensure they work correctly in all scenarios. Also, consider edge cases and potential errors that could occur during execution.

6. Document your functions: Provide clear and concise documentation for your functions, explaining their purpose, input parameters, return values, and any potential side effects. This will make it easier for others to understand and use your functions in their queries.

7. Handle NULL values: Be aware of how your functions handle NULL values and ensure they return the expected results when encountering NULL inputs.

8. Be mindful of data types: Ensure your functions can handle different data types and perform necessary type conversions when required.

9. Use appropriate error handling: Properly handle errors and exceptions within your functions to prevent unexpected issues during query execution.

10. Keep your functions up to date: Regularly review and update your functions to ensure they remain efficient and relevant. Remove any deprecated or unused functions to keep your database clean and organized.

By following these best practices and tips, you can create effective, efficient, and maintainable user-defined functions that enhance your SQL queries and improve your overall database performance.

Summary

In Chapter 7, we explored further into the world of SQL functions and their many subcategories, which included built-in functions, string functions, date and time functions, numerical functions, conditional functions, and user-defined functions. These functions make it possible for developers to carry out complicated operations, change data, and glean insightful information from their databases.

We started off by getting a grasp on the idea of SQL functions and their significance of them in relation to database management. We investigated built-in functions that are readily available for use, such as string manipulation functions (for example, SUBSTR, LENGTH, UPPER, and LOWER), date and time functions (for example, DATE, TIME, DATETIME, JULIANDAY), numeric functions (for example, ABS, ROUND, FLOOR, and CEIL), and conditional functions (for example, CASE, COALESCE, and NULLIF). Following that, we got some hands-on experience with the 'example.db' database to better understand how to implement these methods in SQL queries. In this lesson, we went through a variety of string methods that are useful for searching, extracting, and manipulating text data. In addition, we covered date and time functions, which make it possible for us to carry out operations such as formatting dates, calculating intervals, and extracting particular date and time components. After that, we talked about different mathematical processes and how to round numbers using different numeric functions. In addition, we investigated conditional functions, which make it possible to create more complicated inquiries by permitting the inclusion of conditional expressions within a query.

We also became familiar with the process of creating user-defined functions, often known as UDFs, in order to increase SQLite's capability. UDFs are user-defined functions that may be created in a variety of computer languages, including Python and C, and then loaded into SQLite. We went over the detailed procedure that must be followed in order to develop a UDF with Python and the sqlite3 module, then register the UDF, and finally use it in SQL queries. This gives developers the ability to adapt SQLite's capabilities to suit own requirements, whether those requirements involve performing complicated computations or implementing bespoke business logic. Towards the end, we discussed some best practices and hints for working with SQL functions, such as making use of built-in functions whenever that option is available, ensuring that functions remain uncomplicated and laser-focused, giving functions names that have some sort of significance, ensuring that functions are thoroughly tested, providing clear documentation, managing NULL values, paying attention to data types, employing error handling that is appropriate, and ensuring that functions are kept up to date.

CHAPTER 8: SUBQUERIES AND DERIVED TABLES

In this chapter, we will explore subqueries and derived tables, two important concepts in SQL that allow for more complex and flexible queries. Both subqueries and derived tables help in breaking down complicated queries into smaller, manageable parts and enable the use of intermediate results in other parts of the query.

Overview

Subqueries, also known as nested or inner queries, are SQL queries embedded within another, larger query. They are a powerful tool for structuring complex queries and are typically enclosed in parentheses. Subqueries can be incorporated into various parts of a larger query, including the SELECT, FROM, WHERE, or HAVING clauses, to filter, aggregate, or transform data based on the results of the subquery.

Subqueries are useful for several reasons:

- Simplification: By breaking down complex queries into smaller, more manageable parts, subqueries can make it easier to understand and maintain the query.

- Reusability: Subqueries can be used multiple times within a single query, reducing code redundancy.

- Modularity: Subqueries allow you to encapsulate specific logic or calculations, making it easier to update or change parts of the query without affecting the rest of the query.

Derived tables, on the other hand, are temporary tables created during the execution of a query. They are the result of a SELECT statement embedded within the FROM clause of another query.

Derived tables are useful for several reasons:

- Intermediate results: Derived tables can be used to store intermediate results that are required for further processing in the main query.

- Simplification: Similar to subqueries, derived tables can help simplify complex queries by breaking them down into smaller parts.

- Better performance: In some cases, using derived tables can lead to better query performance, as the database management system may optimize the execution of the query.

While subqueries and derived tables serve similar purposes in terms of simplifying complex queries, they are used in different parts of the query and offer different levels of flexibility. In the following sections, we will explore practical examples of using subqueries and derived tables to manipulate and analyze data more effectively.

Subquery Types

There are several types of subqueries, including scalar subqueries, single-row subqueries, multi-row subqueries, and correlated subqueries. Let us explore each of these types and demonstrate their practical use on the example.db.

Scalar Subquery

A scalar subquery returns a single value (one row and one column). It can be used wherever a single value expression is allowed, such as in the SELECT, WHERE, or HAVING clauses.

Example 1: Find the total number of orders placed.

```
SELECT COUNT(*) FROM orders;
```

Using a scalar subquery, we can find the customers who placed the most orders.

```
SELECT * FROM customers WHERE id = (SELECT customer_id FROM orders GROUP BY customer_id ORDER BY COUNT(*) DESC LIMIT 1);
```

Single-row Subquery

A single-row subquery returns one row with multiple columns. It is used with single-row operators such as =, <>, >, <, >=, and <=.

Example 1: Find the customer with the highest total spending.

```
SELECT c.*, SUM(o.total) AS total_spent
FROM customers c
JOIN orders o ON c.id = o.customer_id
GROUP BY c.id
HAVING total_spent = (SELECT MAX(total_spent) FROM (SELECT SUM(total) AS total_spent FROM orders GROUP BY customer_id) AS subquery);
```

<u>Multi-row Subquery</u>

A multi-row subquery returns multiple rows with a single column. It is used with multi-row operators like IN, ANY, and ALL.

Example 1: Find all orders placed by customers from a specific city.

```
SELECT * FROM orders WHERE customer_id IN (SELECT id FROM customers
WHERE city = 'New York');
```

Example 2: Find all products that have been ordered.

```
SELECT * FROM products WHERE id IN (SELECT DISTINCT product_id
FROM order_items);
```

<u>Correlated Subquery</u>

A correlated subquery is a subquery that depends on the outer query for its values. It is executed once for each row in the outer query. Correlated subqueries can be used in the SELECT, WHERE, and HAVING clauses.

Example 1: Find all customers who have placed more than the average number of orders.

```
SELECT c.*
FROM customers c
WHERE (SELECT COUNT(*) FROM orders o WHERE o.customer_id = c.id) >
(SELECT AVG(order_count) FROM (SELECT COUNT(*) AS order_count FROM
orders GROUP BY customer_id) AS subquery);
```

In these examples, we experienced that these subqueries allow you to write more complex and flexible queries to extract valuable information from your data.

EXISTS and NOT EXISTS

EXISTS and NOT EXISTS are operators used with subqueries to check for the existence of rows in the subquery's result set. EXISTS returns TRUE if the subquery returns at least one row, whereas NOT EXISTS returns TRUE if the subquery returns no rows.

EXISTS

The EXISTS operator is used in combination with a subquery to check if any rows match the specified condition.

Example 1: Find all customers who have placed at least one order.

```
SELECT *
FROM customers c
WHERE EXISTS (SELECT 1 FROM orders o WHERE o.customer_id = c.id);
```

In the above sample program, we're looking for customers with at least one order in the orders table. The subquery checks if there's a matching customer_id in the orders table for the current customer in the outer query. If at least one row is found, EXISTS returns TRUE, and the customer row is included in the result.

NOT EXISTS

The NOT EXISTS operator is used in combination with a subquery to check if no rows match the specified condition.

Example 1: Find all customers who have not placed any orders.

```
SELECT *
FROM customers c
WHERE NOT EXISTS (SELECT 1 FROM orders o WHERE o.customer_id =
c.id);
```

In the above sample program, we're looking for customers without any orders in the orders table. The subquery checks if there's a matching customer_id in the orders table for the current customer in the outer query. If no rows are found, NOT EXISTS returns TRUE, and the customer row is included in the result.

You are possible to filter the data depending on the presence or absence of related data in other tables by using the EXISTS and NOT EXISTS operators in conjunction with subqueries. These operators can be used in the WHERE or HAVING clauses, which will enable you construct more complicated searches to extract information from your database.

IN and NOT IN

IN and NOT IN are operators used with subqueries to compare a single value to a list of values returned by a subquery. IN returns TRUE if the value is found within the list of values, while NOT IN returns TRUE if the value is not found in the list of values.

IN

The IN operator is used to check if a value is present in a list of values or the result of a subquery.

Example 1: Find all customers who live in 'New York', 'Los Angeles', or 'Chicago'.

```
SELECT *
FROM customers
WHERE city IN ('New York', 'Los Angeles', 'Chicago');
```

Example 2: Find all orders placed by customers from the 'USA'.

```
SELECT *
FROM orders
WHERE customer_id IN (SELECT id FROM customers WHERE country =
'USA');
```

In the above sample program, the subquery retrieves a list of customer IDs for customers in the 'USA'. The main query then selects all orders where the customer_id is present in the list returned by the subquery.

NOT IN

The NOT IN operator is used to check if a value is not present in a list of values or the result of a subquery.

Example 1: Find all customers who do not live in 'New York', 'Los Angeles', or 'Chicago'.

```
SELECT *
FROM customers
WHERE city NOT IN ('New York', 'Los Angeles', 'Chicago');
```

Example 2: Find all orders not placed by customers from the 'USA'.

```sql
SELECT *
FROM orders
WHERE customer_id NOT IN (SELECT id FROM customers WHERE country =
'USA');
```

In the above sample program, the subquery retrieves a list of customer IDs for customers in the 'USA'. The main query then selects all orders where the customer_id is not present in the list returned by the subquery.

Using IN and NOT IN operators with subqueries allows you to filter data based on the presence or absence of values in a list or subquery results.

Common Table Expressions (CTEs)

Exploring CTEs

Common Table Expressions (CTEs) are a powerful feature in SQL that allows you to create a temporary result set, which you can then reference within a SELECT, INSERT, UPDATE, or DELETE statement. CTEs are especially useful for breaking down complex queries into simpler, more readable parts.

To define a CTE, you use the WITH keyword followed by the name you want to give to the CTE and an optional list of column names. Then, you specify the query that defines the CTE result set.

Below is a sample program to demonstrate the use of a CTE with the example.db database:

Sample Program

Lets practice an example wherein we will try to find the total sales amount for each customer.

Step 1: Create a CTE that calculates the total sales amount for each order.

```sql
WITH order_totals AS (
  SELECT
    order_id,
```

```
    SUM(quantity * price) AS total_amount
  FROM
    order_items
  GROUP BY
    order_id
)
SELECT
  *
FROM
  order_totals;
```

Step 2: Use the CTE to find the total sales amount for each customer.

```
WITH order_totals AS (
  SELECT
    order_id,
    SUM(quantity * pricc) AS total_amount
  FROM
    order_items
  GROUP BY
    order_id
)
SELECT
  c.id AS customer_id,
  c.name AS customer_name,
  SUM(ot.total_amount) AS total_sales_amount
FROM
  customers c
  JOIN orders o ON c.id = o.customer_id
  JOIN order_totals ot ON o.id = ot.order_id
GROUP BY
  c.id;
```

In the above sample program, we first create a CTE named order_totals that calculates the total sales amount for each order. Then, we use the CTE in the main query to find the total sales amount for each customer by joining the customers, orders, and order_totals tables.

CTEs can be used to create more readable queries by breaking them down into smaller, more manageable parts. They can also be used to create recursive queries, which are queries that reference themselves to solve hierarchical or iterative problems.

Recursive CTEs

Recursive Common Table Expressions (CTEs) are valuable tools in SQL queries when addressing hierarchical or iterative problems, as they provide an efficient and concise method for handling complex data structures. With the ability to reference the CTE within its own definition, recursive CTEs enable traversal through hierarchical data structures such as organizational charts, nested categories, or tree-like structures. This powerful technique allows for dynamic, self-referencing queries, simplifying the process of working with multi-level relationships, parent-child relationships, and other recursive data patterns. By utilizing recursive CTEs, developers can achieve enhanced readability, maintainability, and performance in their SQL queries.

To create a recursive CTE, you define an "anchor query" that provides the base result set and a "recursive query" that references the CTE and adds rows to the result set based on the anchor query's results. These two queries are separated by the UNION or UNION ALL operator.

Below is a sample program to demonstrate the use of a recursive CTE with the example.db database:

Example: Find all employees and their managers in an organization, assuming there is a table named "employees" with columns "id", "name", "manager_id".

Step 1: Create a recursive CTE that finds all employees and their managers.

```
WITH RECURSIVE employee_hierarchy AS (
  -- Anchor query: Select all employees who don't have a manager (top level)
  SELECT
    e.id,
    e.name,
    e.manager_id,
```

```sql
    NULL AS manager_name,
    1 AS level
  FROM
    employees e
  WHERE
    e.manager_id IS NULL

  UNION ALL
  -- Recursive query: Select employees and their managers based on the previous level

  SELECT
    e.id,
    e.name,
    e.manager_id,
    eh.name AS manager_name,
    eh.level + 1 AS level
  FROM
    employees e
    JOIN employee_hierarchy eh ON e.manager_id = eh.id
)
SELECT
  *
FROM
  employee_hierarchy
ORDER BY
  level;
```

In the above sample program, the anchor query selects all employees who don't have a manager, which represents the top level of the organization. The recursive query then selects employees and their managers based on the previous level in the hierarchy. The "level" column is used to track the depth of the hierarchy.

The result of this query will be a list of all employees in the organization, along with their manager's name and the level in the hierarchy. Keep in mind that recursive CTEs can be resource-intensive, so it's essential to use them judiciously and ensure that the recursion has a proper termination condition.

Derived Tables

Derived tables are temporary tables that are created and used only within the scope of a single SQL query. They can be used to simplify complex queries, break down large queries into smaller, more manageable parts, or encapsulate a portion of the query logic that you want to reuse in multiple places within the query. Derived tables can be created using subqueries in the FROM clause, Common Table Expressions (CTEs), or by using inline views.

Subquery in FROM Clause

Using a subquery in the FROM clause allows you to create a derived table that can be used in the rest of the query. Below is a sample program using the "orders" and "order_items" tables from example.db:

```
SELECT
  dt.customer_id,
  SUM(dt.total_price) as total_spent
FROM
  (
   SELECT
     o.customer_id,
     o.id as order_id,
     SUM(oi.price * oi.quantity) as total_price
   FROM
     orders o
     JOIN order_items oi ON o.id = oi.order_id
   GROUP BY
     o.customer_id,
     o.id
  ) dt
 GROUP BY
  dt.customer_id
 ORDER BY
```

total_spent DESC;

In the above sample program, we create a derived table (dt) using a subquery in the FROM clause. The subquery calculates the total price for each order, and the outer query calculates the total amount spent by each customer.

Common Table Expressions

CTEs can also be used to create derived tables that are reusable within the query. The given below is the same example as above, but using a CTE:

```
WITH order_totals AS (
  SELECT
    o.customer_id,
    o.id as order_id,
    SUM(oi.price * oi.quantity) as total_price
  FROM
    orders o
    JOIN order_items oi ON o.id = oi.order_id
  GROUP BY
    o.customer_id,
    o.id
)
SELECT
  customer_id,
  SUM(total_price) as total_spent
FROM
  order_totals
GROUP BY
  customer_id
ORDER BY
  total_spent DESC;
```

Inline Views

An inline view is a subquery in the FROM clause that has an alias, which can be used to reference columns from the subquery in the outer query. Inline views are similar to subqueries in the FROM clause, but they are explicitly given a name. This name can make your query easier to read and understand.

Below is a sample program using inline views with the "products" table from example.db:

```
SELECT
  category,
  AVG(price) as avg_price
FROM
  (SELECT p.category, p.price FROM products p) AS inline_view
GROUP BY
  category;
```

In the above sample program, we create an inline view named "inline_view" using a subquery in the FROM clause. The subquery selects the "category" and "price" columns from the "products" table. The outer query then calculates the average price for each category.

Derived Tables Best Practices

Now that we've explored various types of derived tables, let us look at some best practices and tips when using them:

- Use derived tables to simplify complex queries: Break down large queries into smaller, more manageable parts by encapsulating portions of the query logic in derived tables. This can make your SQL code more readable and maintainable.

- Use derived tables for reusable query logic: If you have a portion of a query that needs to be reused in multiple places within the same query, consider using a derived table, such as a CTE. This can help avoid duplicate code and make your query easier to understand.

- Be mindful of performance: While derived tables can simplify your queries and make them more readable, they may also introduce performance overhead. The database system may need to materialize the derived table before executing the outer query, which can lead to increased processing time and memory usage. However, some database systems are smart enough to optimize the execution of derived tables, so the impact on performance may vary depending on the specific database system you're using.

- Use appropriate derived table types: Choose the type of derived table that best suits your needs. For example, if you need a temporary table that's reusable within a single query, consider using a CTE. If you need a simple inline view to reference columns from a subquery in the outer query, consider using an inline view with an alias.

- Be careful with recursive queries: When using recursive CTEs, ensure that you have a proper termination condition to avoid infinite loops, which can lead to poor performance or even crash your database system. Always test your recursive queries thoroughly before deploying them in a production environment.

Overall, derived tables can be a powerful tool for simplifying complex queries, encapsulating reusable query logic, and breaking down large queries into smaller, more manageable parts.

Summary

In this Chapter, we explored the concepts of subqueries and derived tables in detail. Subqueries are queries embedded within other queries, allowing us to utilize the result of an inner query within an outer query. We learned about the different types of subqueries, such as scalar subqueries, multi-valued subqueries, and correlated subqueries. Practical demonstrations using the example.db database helped in understanding their real world applications. We also delved into EXISTS and NOT EXISTS clauses, which are used to test the existence of records in a subquery. The IN and NOT IN clauses were discussed, which are used to filter data based on a list of values returned by a subquery. These concepts were further illustrated with examples using the example.db database.

Common Table Expressions (CTEs) were introduced as a technique for creating temporary, reusable tables within a single query. We learned how to create recursive queries using CTEs, which are useful for traversing hierarchical data structures like organizational charts and parent-child relationships. Careful attention must be paid to termination conditions in recursive queries to avoid infinite loops and performance issues. Derived tables, which are temporary tables created within a query, were also covered. We discussed their types and demonstrated each of them using the example.db database. Derived tables can simplify complex queries, encapsulate reusable query logic, and break down large queries into smaller, more manageable parts.

Lastly, we provided best practices and tips for using derived tables, emphasizing the importance of simplifying complex queries, reusing query logic, being mindful of performance, using appropriate derived table types, and being careful with recursive queries. These guidelines help ensure efficient, readable, and maintainable SQL code.

CHAPTER 9: VIEWS AND MATERIALIZED VIEWS

Overview

In this Chapter, we will delve into the concepts of views and materialized views in SQL, which are essential for SQL developers to understand and utilize effectively. Lets understand Views and they are nothing but virtual tables derived from the result set of a SELECT statement. They do not store data themselves but represent a predefined query that can be executed upon request.

Views offer several advantages to SQL developers:

Simplification: Views encapsulate complex queries into a single, reusable object, which simplifies the SQL code. Instead of writing the same lengthy query multiple times, developers can create a view and reference it in their queries. This results in easier-to-read and maintain code.

Security: Views can be used to restrict access to specific columns or rows in a table, enhancing data security. By granting users permission to access a view, developers can control the data they are authorized to see without modifying the underlying table structure or data.

Abstraction: Views provide a layer of abstraction between the data and the end-users or applications. This allows developers to make changes to the underlying table structure without affecting users or applications that rely on the views. This flexibility can be invaluable when managing a constantly evolving database schema.

Modularity: Views promote modular design by breaking down complex queries into smaller, more manageable components. This approach can improve query performance, readability, and maintainability.

Materialized views are similar to views, but they store the result set of the underlying query in a separate table. This key difference provides performance advantages because the data is precomputed and readily available when a query is executed against the materialized view. However, this also means that the data in the materialized view might not always be up-to-date with the base tables, requiring additional maintenance tasks, such as refreshing the materialized view.

Further in this chapter, we will examine the following topics in-depth:

Creating views: Learn how to define and create views using the CREATE VIEW statement, and how to use them in your queries.

Modifying views: Explore how to alter the structure or definition of a view using the ALTER

VIEW statement and how to drop a view using the DROP VIEW statement.

Materialized views: Understand the concept of materialized views, their benefits, and drawbacks, and how to create, refresh, and manage them using the appropriate SQL statements.

Indexing views: Discover how to create indexes on views to further improve query performance.

Security and permissions: Learn about managing access control and permissions related to views and materialized views.

As we progress through this chapter, we will provide detailed explanations and practical examples using the example.db, ensuring that early SQL developers can grasp and apply these essential concepts effectively.

Creating and Managing Views

Creating a view in a database is an effortless process that requires the utilization of the CREATE VIEW statement. This statement is accompanied by the desired view's name, the AS keyword, and the SELECT statement, which outlines the view's structure. To demonstrate this concept, we will use the example.db as our reference. By employing views, we can effectively organize and manage data, streamlining the process of retrieving and displaying specific information from complex queries or multiple tables. This method promotes efficiency and simplicity in managing and accessing data in a database system.

Consider the following schema in example.db:
1. students (id, first_name, last_name, age, grade_level)
2. courses (id, course_name, instructor_id)
3. instructors (id, first_name, last_name)
4. enrollments (student_id, course_id)

Now, let us create a view that lists all students with their full names:

```
CREATE VIEW full_name_students AS
SELECT id, first_name || ' ' || last_name AS full_name, age, grade_level
FROM students;
```

To query the view, you can use it just like a regular table:

```sql
SELECT full_name, age, grade_level
FROM full_name_students;
```

Next, let us create a view that displays the list of courses along with the instructor's full name:

```sql
CREATE VIEW courses_with_instructors AS
SELECT c.id, c.course_name, i.first_name || ' ' || i.last_name AS
instructor_full_name
FROM courses c
JOIN instructors i ON c.instructor_id = i.id;
```

You can now query the courses_with_instructors view:

```sql
SELECT course_name, instructor_full_name
FROM courses_with_instructors;
```

Finally, let us create a view that lists all students along with the courses they are enrolled in:

```sql
CREATE VIEW student_course_enrollments AS
SELECT s.id, s.first_name || ' ' || s.last_name AS full_name, c.course_name
FROM students s
JOIN enrollments e ON s.id = e.student_id
JOIN courses c ON e.course_id = c.id;
```

To get the list of students and their enrolled courses, you can query the view as follows:

```sql
SELECT full_name, course_name
FROM student_course_enrollments;
```

These examples demonstrate how views can simplify queries and encapsulate complex logic, making it easier to reuse and maintain your SQL code.

Modifying Views

Modifying views in a database is essential for maintaining accurate and up-to-date representations of the underlying data. This process involves changing the structure or updating the SELECT statement that defines the view. However, in SQLite, you cannot directly modify a view using the ALTER VIEW statement as you might in other database systems. To modify a view in SQLite, you need to first drop the existing view using the DROP VIEW statement, effectively deleting it. Once the view has been removed, you can then recreate it with the desired modifications to the SELECT statement by employing the CREATE VIEW statement. This two-step process ensures that your SQLite view remains current and accurately reflects any changes to the data or required structure.

Let us consider the previous examples from example.db, and suppose you want to modify the full_name_students view to also include the student's email addresses. First, you need to drop the existing view:

```
DROP VIEW IF EXISTS full_name_students;
```

Next, recreate the view with the modified SELECT statement that includes the email column:

```
CREATE VIEW full_name_students AS
SELECT id, first_name || ' ' || last_name AS full_name, age, grade_level, email
FROM students;
```

Now, the full_name_students view includes the email addresses of the students.

Keep in mind that dropping and recreating views may lead to dependencies issues if other views or queries depend on the view being modified. Be cautious when modifying views, and ensure that you update any dependent objects accordingly.

Let us consider another example using the courses and enrollments tables in the example.db. Suppose you want to create a view that shows the total number of enrolled students for each course.

Initially, you create the view as follows:

```
CREATE VIEW course_enrollment_count AS
SELECT c.id AS course_id, c.name AS course_name, COUNT(e.student_id) AS
```

```sql
enrollment_count
FROM courses c
JOIN enrollments e ON c.id = e.course_id
GROUP BY c.id;
```

Now, let us assume that you want to modify the view to include the course's start date. You will first drop the existing view and then recreate it with the modified SELECT statement.

Drop the existing view:

```sql
DROP VIEW IF EXISTS course_enrollment_count;
```

Recreate the view with the modified SELECT statement:

```sql
CREATE VIEW course_enrollment_count AS
SELECT c.id AS course_id, c.name AS course_name, c.start_date,
COUNT(e.student_id) AS enrollment_count
FROM courses c
JOIN enrollments e ON c.id = e.course_id
GROUP BY c.id;
```

Now, the course_enrollment_count view includes the start date of each course along with the enrollment count.

Be cautious when modifying views, as other dependent objects may need to be updated. The approach demonstrated above is specific to SQLite. Other database management systems may offer different methods for modifying views, such as the ALTER VIEW statement which exists in SQL Server and PostgreSQL.

Materialized Views

Materialized views are a more advanced feature available in some database management systems, but not in SQLite. Nonetheless, it's essential to understand the concept as it can be beneficial when working with other databases like PostgreSQL, Oracle, or SQL Server.

A materialized view is similar to a regular view, but instead of storing only the SQL query, it stores the actual result of the query. This means that the data in a materialized view is static and only refreshed when explicitly requested. Materialized views can significantly improve query performance, especially for complex or resource-intensive queries, as the data is precomputed and stored.

To create a materialized view in a database management system that supports it, you would typically use the CREATE MATERIALIZED VIEW statement. For example, in PostgreSQL, you could create a materialized view like this:

```
CREATE MATERIALIZED VIEW course_enrollment_count AS
SELECT c.id AS course_id, c.name AS course_name, COUNT(e.student_id) AS
enrollment_count
FROM courses c
JOIN enrollments e ON c.id = e.course_id
GROUP BY c.id;
```

Once created, you can query the materialized view just like any other table or view. Keep in mind that the data in the materialized view will not be updated automatically. To refresh the data, you will need to use the REFRESH MATERIALIZED VIEW statement:

```
REFRESH MATERIALIZED VIEW course_enrollment_count;
```

This statement updates the materialized view's data by re-executing the underlying query and storing the new result. Depending on the database management system, you might have options to refresh the materialized view incrementally (only updating the changed data) or to refresh it in the background (allowing for concurrent reads).

Please remember that materialized views are not available in SQLite, but it's essential to be aware of this concept so let us consider another example using the PostgreSQL database management system. Assume that we have two tables in our example.db: products and sales. The products table contains information about the products, while the sales table stores sales data for each product.

Below is a sample program of these tables:

products table:

id	name
1	Product A
2	Product B
3	Product C

sales table:

id	product_id	quantity	sale_date
1	1	10	2023-01-01
2	1	5	2023-01-15
3	2	8	2023-01-20
4	3	20	2023-02-05
5	1	12	2023-02-10

Now, let us assume that we want to create a materialized view to store the total quantity sold for each product. We would use the following SQL statement in PostgreSQL:

```sql
CREATE MATERIALIZED VIEW product_total_sales AS
SELECT p.id AS product_id, p.name AS product_name, SUM(s.quantity) AS
total_quantity
FROM products p
JOIN sales s ON p.id = s.product_id
GROUP BY p.id, p.name;
```

The materialized view product_total_sales now contains the precomputed total quantity for each product:

product_id	product_name	total_quantity
1	Product A	27
2	Product B	8
3	Product C	20

Remember that the data in the materialized view is static and will not update automatically when new sales records are added. To refresh the materialized view, you would need to execute the REFRESH MATERIALIZED VIEW statement:

```
REFRESH MATERIALIZED VIEW product_total_sales;
```

Again, please keep in mind that this example uses PostgreSQL, as SQLite does not support materialized views.

Security and Permissions

SQLite does not have an elaborate built-in access control mechanism like other RDBMS. However, it provides basic access control through file system permissions on the database files themselves.

In more sophisticated RDBMS like PostgreSQL, MySQL, and SQL Server, you can manage access control and permissions related to views and materialized views. The given below is a general overview of managing permissions in these systems, although the syntax and specific features may vary:

Granting Permissions

You can grant permissions such as SELECT, INSERT, UPDATE, and DELETE to specific users or roles on views or materialized views. For example, granting SELECT permission to a user named user1 on a view named my_view:

PostgreSQL / MySQL:

```
GRANT SELECT ON my_view TO user1;
```

SQL Server:

```
GRANT SELECT ON my_view TO user1;
```

Revoking Permissions

To revoke permissions, you can use the REVOKE statement. For example, revoking SELECT permission from user1 on my_view:

PostgreSQL / MySQL:

```
REVOKE SELECT ON my_view FROM user1;
```

SQL Server:

```
REVOKE SELECT ON my_view FROM user1;
```

With Check Option

When creating a view, you can use the WITH CHECK OPTION to ensure that any data modifications through the view conform to the view's filter conditions. This can be useful for enforcing data integrity when users have write permissions on a view.

```
CREATE VIEW my_filtered_view AS
SELECT * FROM my_table
WHERE some_condition
WITH CHECK OPTION;
```

We can use the above examples provided as a starting point to explore access control and permissions in database systems like PostgreSQL, MySQL, and SQL Server.

Summary

In Chapter 9, we explored Views and Materialized Views, which are essential tools for SQL developers. Views are virtual tables that represent the result of a SELECT query. They simplify complex queries, enhance security, and promote code reusability. Materialized views, on the other hand, store the result of a query physically, providing performance improvements for read-heavy workloads.

We started by learning how to create views using the CREATE VIEW statement. Views can be created based on a SELECT query, and they allow developers to abstract the underlying table structure. This simplifies queries, making them more readable and maintainable. We demonstrated the creation of views using example.db.

Next, we discussed modifying views. In some RDBMS, you can use the CREATE OR REPLACE VIEW statement to modify an existing view without affecting the dependent objects. We provided examples of modifying views based on example.db. We then covered Materialized Views, which store the result of a query physically, unlike regular views that recompute the result every time they are accessed. Materialized views offer performance advantages for read-heavy workloads, as they don't need to re-execute the underlying query. However, they come with the trade-off of increased storage requirements and the need to refresh the data periodically. We demonstrated the creation of materialized views using examples based on example.db.

Following that, we delved into view indexing, which can significantly improve query performance. Indexing views allows the database engine to quickly locate the relevant rows when executing a query, reducing the overall response time. We provided two examples of view indexing using example.db. Lastly, we discussed security and permissions related to views and materialized views. Although SQLite does not have a built-in access control mechanism, other RDBMS like PostgreSQL, MySQL, and SQL Server provide robust options for managing permissions. We reviewed granting and revoking permissions, as well as the WITH CHECK OPTION to enforce data integrity when users have write permissions on a view.

Chapter 10: Advanced SQL Topics

Overview

In this chapter, we will delve into advanced SQL topics, including transactions, triggers, and index optimization. These advanced concepts play a crucial role in ensuring data consistency, automating specific actions, and optimizing database performance, all of which are essential for business applications.

Transactions are a series of SQL statements that are executed as a single unit of work. They ensure that either all the statements in the unit are successfully executed, or none of them are, maintaining the database's consistency and integrity. Transactions follow the ACID properties: Atomicity, Consistency, Isolation, and Durability. Atomicity guarantees that all statements within a transaction are either committed or rolled back. Consistency ensures that the database remains in a consistent state before and after the transaction. Isolation means that each transaction is isolated from others, preventing interference. Durability ensures that committed changes persist even in the case of system failure. Triggers are automated actions that the database executes in response to specific events, such as INSERT, UPDATE, DELETE, or a combination of these events. Triggers can be used for various purposes, including maintaining referential integrity, enforcing business rules, auditing changes, and replicating data. By using triggers, businesses can automate essential tasks and ensure that specific actions occur whenever specific conditions are met. Index optimization is a crucial aspect of database performance tuning. Indexes can significantly improve the performance of SELECT queries by allowing the database engine to quickly locate the relevant rows. However, they can also negatively impact the performance of INSERT, UPDATE, and DELETE operations, as the database must maintain the indexes alongside the data. Therefore, it is crucial to strike a balance between creating useful indexes and avoiding over-indexing. Index optimization techniques, such as choosing the right index type, using covering indexes, and periodically analyzing and rebuilding indexes, can help businesses achieve optimal database performance.

This chapter will cover advanced SQL concepts, focusing on transactions, triggers, and index optimization. These concepts are essential for maintaining data consistency, automating actions, and optimizing performance in business applications.

Transactions and ACID

Transactions in SQL are crucial for maintaining database consistency and integrity, as they involve executing a series of statements as a single unit of work. This means that if all the statements within the transaction are successfully executed, the changes are committed and made permanent. However, if any statement within the transaction fails, the entire transaction is rolled back, and no changes are made to the database. This ensures data reliability, as transactions follow the ACID properties, which include Atomicity, Consistency, Isolation, and Durability. By grouping multiple statements into a single transaction, SQL enables better control over complex operations and error handling, ultimately improving overall database performance and stability.

Transactions follow the ACID properties: Atomicity, Consistency, Isolation, and Durability.

Atomicity: It guarantees that all statements within a transaction are either committed or rolled back. If any statement in the transaction fails, the entire transaction is rolled back, and no changes are made to the database.

Consistency: It ensures that the database remains in a consistent state before and after the transaction. The transaction moves the database from one consistent state to another.

Isolation: It means that each transaction is isolated from others, preventing interference. Concurrent transactions appear as if they were executed sequentially.

Durability: It ensures that committed changes persist even in the case of system failure. Once a transaction is committed, its effects are permanently stored in the database.

Exploring ACID in Practice

Let us create a sample SQL database to understand ACID properties in action. We will create two tables: 'accounts' and 'transactions'.

```sql
CREATE TABLE accounts (
    id INTEGER PRIMARY KEY,
    name TEXT NOT NULL,
    balance DECIMAL(10, 2) NOT NULL
);
```

```sql
CREATE TABLE transactions (
    id INTEGER PRIMARY KEY,
    account_id INTEGER NOT NULL,
    amount DECIMAL(10, 2) NOT NULL,
    FOREIGN KEY (account_id) REFERENCES accounts(id)
);
```

Now, let us insert sample data into the 'accounts' table:

```sql
INSERT INTO accounts (id, name, balance) VALUES (1, 'Alice', 1000);
INSERT INTO accounts (id, name, balance) VALUES (2, 'Bob', 1000);
```

Suppose we want to transfer 200 from Alice's account to Bob's account. We can use a transaction to make sure the transfer is atomic, consistent, isolated, and durable:

```sql
BEGIN TRANSACTION;

-- Decrease Alice's balance by 200
UPDATE accounts SET balance = balance - 200 WHERE id = 1;

-- Increase Bob's balance by 200
UPDATE accounts SET balance = balance + 200 WHERE id = 2;

-- Add a record to the transactions table
INSERT INTO transactions (account_id, amount) VALUES (1, -200);
INSERT INTO transactions (account_id, amount) VALUES (2, 200);

COMMIT;
```

The given below is a detailed explanation of each step of the transaction:

BEGIN TRANSACTION;: This statement marks the start of a new transaction. From this point onwards, all the subsequent SQL statements will be part of this transaction.

UPDATE accounts SET balance = balance - 200 WHERE id = 1;: This statement reduces Alice's account balance by 200. Since her account ID is 1, we use a WHERE clause to target her account. The balance is updated by subtracting 200 from the current balance.

UPDATE accounts SET balance = balance + 200 WHERE id = 2;: This statement increases Bob's account balance by 200. We target Bob's account using the WHERE clause (his account ID is 2). The balance is updated by adding 200 to the current balance.

INSERT INTO transactions (account_id, amount) VALUES (1, -200);: This statement records the transaction in the 'transactions' table. We insert a new row, associating the transaction with Alice's account ID (1) and setting the amount to -200, indicating a withdrawal.

INSERT INTO transactions (account_id, amount) VALUES (2, 200);: Similarly, we record the transaction for Bob's account by inserting a new row in the 'transactions' table. We associate the transaction with Bob's account ID (2) and set the amount to 200, indicating a deposit.

COMMIT;: This statement marks the end of the transaction and commits all the changes made during the transaction. If all the statements within the transaction are executed successfully, the changes will be permanently stored in the database. In case of an error or failure in any statement, the entire transaction would be rolled back, and no changes would be made to the database.

Using a transaction ensures that the entire operation is atomic (either all changes are committed or none), consistent (database remains in a consistent state before and after the transaction), isolated (preventing interference from other concurrent transactions), and durable (committed changes persist even in the case of system failure).

Stored Procedures and Functions

Stored Procedures

Stored procedures are pre-compiled, reusable SQL code segments that can perform a specific task or a series of tasks. They can be called and executed by the client applications. Stored procedures provide a way to modularize and encapsulate database operations, improve performance by reducing network traffic, and maintain consistency in implementing business logic.

The given below is a simple example of a stored procedure (using a generic SQL syntax) that transfers funds between two accounts:

```
CREATE PROCEDURE TransferFunds
  @from_account_id INT,
  @to_account_id INT,
  @amount DECIMAL(10, 2)
AS
BEGIN
  BEGIN TRANSACTION;
    UPDATE accounts SET balance = balance - @amount WHERE id =
@from_account_id;
    UPDATE accounts SET balance = balance + @amount WHERE id =
```

```sql
@to_account_id;
    INSERT INTO transactions (account_id, amount) VALUES (@from_account_id,
-@amount);
    INSERT INTO transactions (account_id, amount) VALUES (@to_account_id,
@amount);
  COMMIT;
END;
```

The stored procedure TransferFunds accepts three parameters:
1. @from_account_id: The ID of the account from which the funds will be transferred.
2. @to_account_id: The ID of the account to which the funds will be transferred.
3. @amount: The amount of money to be transferred.

The stored procedure begins by starting a transaction using the BEGIN TRANSACTION; statement. A transaction ensures that all the SQL statements within it are executed as a single unit of work. If any statement fails, the entire transaction is rolled back, and no changes are made to the data.

Next, the procedure updates the balance of the from_account by subtracting the @amount from its current balance. Then, it updates the balance of the to_account by adding the @amount to its current balance.

After updating the account balances, the procedure inserts two records into the transactions table. One record represents the withdrawal from the from_account with a negative amount, and the other record represents the deposit into the to_account with a positive amount.

Finally, the procedure commits the transaction using the COMMIT; statement. If all the statements execute successfully, the changes are permanent. If any statement fails, the transaction is rolled back, and no changes are made to the data.

To call this stored procedure, you'd use the following statement:

```sql
EXEC TransferFunds @from_account_id = 1, @to_account_id = 2, @amount =
200;
```

Stored Functions

Stored functions are similar to stored procedures but with a crucial difference: they return a single value or a table. They can be used within SQL statements just like built-in functions. Stored functions are useful when you need to perform complex calculations or operations and reuse them across multiple queries.

The given below is a simple example of a stored function (using a generic SQL syntax) that calculates the total balance of a specific account type:

```sql
CREATE FUNCTION GetTotalBalanceByAccountType
  (@account_type INT)
RETURNS DECIMAL(10, 2)
AS
BEGIN
  DECLARE @total_balance DECIMAL(10, 2);

  SELECT @total_balance = SUM(balance)
  FROM accounts
  WHERE account_type = @account_type;

  RETURN @total_balance;
END;
```

To call this stored function within a SQL statement, you'd use the following query:

```sql
SELECT dbo.GetTotalBalanceByAccountType(1) AS TotalBalance;
```

The stored function GetTotalBalanceByAccountType accepts one parameter:
- @account_type: The account type for which the total balance should be calculated.

The function declares a variable @total_balance of type DECIMAL(10, 2) to store the calculated total balance.

The SELECT statement calculates the sum of the balance column for all the rows in the accounts table where the account_type matches the input parameter @account_type. The result is stored in the @total_balance variable.

Finally, the function returns the value of the @total_balance variable using the RETURN statement.

When calling this function within a SQL statement, you can use it just like any built-in function. In the example provided, the function is called within a SELECT statement, and the returned total balance is given an alias TotalBalance.

Triggers

When specified events take place, such as INSERT, UPDATE, or DELETE operations being conducted on a particular table or view, triggers are specialized database objects that automatically run a predefined set of SQL statements. Triggers are also known as event handlers. These occurrences set off the trigger, which in turn causes the predetermined actions to be carried out. When it comes to enforcing rules governing data integrity, maintaining referential integrity between linked tables, reviewing data alterations for the sake of security and compliance, and automating repetitive activities, triggers are a useful tool.

Let us assume the following table structure for the account and transactions tables:

```
CREATE TABLE accounts (
    id INTEGER PRIMARY KEY,
    account_type VARCHAR(10),
    balance DECIMAL(10, 2)
);
```

```
CREATE TABLE transactions (
    id INTEGER PRIMARY KEY,
    account_id INTEGER,
    amount DECIMAL(10, 2),
    transaction_date DATETIME,
    FOREIGN KEY (account_id) REFERENCES accounts(id)
);
```

To demonstrate the use of triggers, let us create an AFTER INSERT trigger that automatically inserts a new record into the transactions table every time an account is created:

Create Trigger

```sql
CREATE TRIGGER account_creation_trigger
AFTER INSERT
ON accounts
FOR EACH ROW
BEGIN
   INSERT INTO transactions(account_id, amount, transaction_date)
   VALUES (NEW.id, NEW.balance, CURRENT_TIMESTAMP);
END;
```

This trigger is named account_creation_trigger, and it is executed after an INSERT operation on the accounts table. FOR EACH ROW means that the trigger is executed once for each row affected by the INSERT operation.

Inside the trigger body, we insert a new record into the transactions table, using the NEW keyword to reference the values of the newly inserted row in the accounts table. NEW.id and NEW.balance represent the id and balance values of the new account, and CURRENT_TIMESTAMP represents the current date and time.

Test the Trigger

```sql
INSERT INTO accounts(account_type, balance)
VALUES ('Savings', 1000.00);


SELECT * FROM transactions;
```

When you insert a new account with a balance of 1000.00, the trigger automatically inserts a corresponding record into the transactions table with the same account ID, amount, and the current timestamp.

Triggers can also be used to maintain data integrity or enforce business rules. They can be classified into different types based on the event they respond to and the timing of their execution:
* BEFORE INSERT: Executes before a new row is inserted into a table.
* AFTER INSERT: Executes after a new row is inserted into a table.

- BEFORE UPDATE: Executes before an existing row is updated in a table.
- AFTER UPDATE: Executes after an existing row is updated in a table.
- BEFORE DELETE: Executes before a row is deleted from a table.
- AFTER DELETE: Executes after a row is deleted from a table.

Let us look at another example of using triggers to enforce a business rule. Suppose we have an employees table with the following structure:

```sql
CREATE TABLE employees (
    id INTEGER PRIMARY KEY,
    first_name VARCHAR(50),
    last_name VARCHAR(50),
    salary DECIMAL(10, 2),
    department_id INTEGER
);
```

We want to enforce a rule that states that an employee's salary cannot be decreased. To achieve this, we can create a BEFORE UPDATE trigger:

```sql
CREATE TRIGGER prevent_salary_decrease
BEFORE UPDATE OF salary
ON employees
FOR EACH ROW
WHEN NEW.salary < OLD.salary
BEGIN
    RAISE(FAIL, 'Salary cannot be decreased.');
END;
```

This trigger is named prevent_salary_decrease, and it is executed before an UPDATE operation on the salary column of the employees table. The WHEN clause checks if the new salary (NEW.salary) is less than the old salary (OLD.salary). If the condition is true, the trigger raises an error and prevents the update operation.

Now, let us test the trigger:

```sql
-- Attempting to decrease an employee's salary
```

```
UPDATE employees
SET salary = salary - 500
WHERE id = 1;
```

The trigger will prevent this update from happening, and an error message will be displayed, stating that the salary cannot be decreased.

Index Optimization

The optimization of indexes is a crucial component of the management of SQL databases. This is because index optimization considerably boosts the performance and effectiveness of queries. It is possible to establish an index, which is an object in a database, on a single column or numerous columns contained within a table. This provides the database with the ability to search and retrieve records more quickly and easily. Index optimization, which involves optimizing the search process, enables faster response times and reduces the amount of system resources that are used. It is essential for a database to have careful management of these indexes, which includes generating, updating, and deleting them as needed, in order to maintain its flexibility and operate at its optimal level of performance. This not only improves the performance of the system as a whole, but it also adds to a better user experience because it allows queries to be run and results to be shown with a minimal amount of delay.

Creating Index

Let us use our previous employees table as an example. Suppose we frequently query the table based on the department_id column. Without an index, the database would have to perform a full table scan to find the matching rows, which can be slow, especially for large tables. By creating an index on the department_id column, we can significantly speed up such queries.

To create an index on the department_id column, you can execute the following SQL statement:

```
CREATE INDEX idx_department_id ON employees (department_id);
```

Now, when you run a query that filters by department_id, the database will use the index to quickly find the relevant rows, resulting in faster query execution.

However, keep in mind that indexes come with some trade-offs. While they can speed up SELECT queries, they can also slow down INSERT, UPDATE, and DELETE operations, as the database needs to maintain the index structure. Moreover, indexes consume additional storage space. Thus, it's essential to strike a balance between the benefits and costs of using indexes.

Best Practices for Index Optimization

Some general guidelines for index optimization are:

- Create indexes on columns that are frequently used in WHERE clauses or JOIN conditions.
- Limit the number of indexes on a table, as having too many indexes can negatively impact the performance of data modification operations.
- Avoid creating indexes on columns with a low cardinality (i.e., a small number of distinct values), as they may not provide a significant performance improvement.
- Regularly analyze your database's performance and usage patterns, and make adjustments to your indexing strategy as needed.

In summary, index optimization is about creating and managing indexes to improve query performance without incurring excessive overhead in terms of storage space and data modification operations. By following best practices and regularly monitoring your database, you can achieve an optimal balance between performance and resource usage.

Query Performance Tuning

Query performance tuning is the process of optimizing SQL queries to enhance their execution time and minimize the strain on the database system. This critical practice involves analyzing individual queries, examining their structure, and identifying potential bottlenecks that may impede their efficiency. By making strategic adjustments to the queries, such as rewriting them, indexing relevant columns, or optimizing the database schema, database administrators and developers can significantly improve performance. Ultimately, effective query performance tuning leads to faster query results, more efficient resource utilization, and improved overall system responsiveness, which benefits both end users and organizations relying on the database system.

There are several techniques you can employ to optimize query performance, including:

- Use indexes: As discussed earlier, creating indexes on frequently queried columns can significantly speed up SELECT queries. Do not forget to create appropriate indexes based on your database usage patterns.

- Limit the result set: Retrieve only the required data by specifying the necessary columns in the SELECT clause and using WHERE conditions to filter the data.

- Avoid using SELECT: Selecting all columns from a table can lead to unnecessary data retrieval and slow down query execution. Instead, list the specific columns you need in the SELECT clause.

- Use JOINs instead of subqueries: In some cases, using JOINs can be more efficient than using subqueries, especially when working with large data sets.

- Optimize JOINs: Choose the most appropriate type of JOIN (e.g., INNER JOIN, OUTER JOIN) based on your requirements. Additionally, try to minimize the number of JOINs in a single query, as they can significantly impact performance.

- Use aggregate functions and GROUP BY: When you need to perform calculations on grouped data, use aggregate functions (COUNT, SUM, AVG, MIN, MAX) in combination with the GROUP BY clause.

- Optimize the use of functions: Avoid using functions on indexed columns in the WHERE clause, as this can prevent the database from using the index. If possible, rewrite the query to use functions on non-indexed columns or constant values.

- Analyze query execution plans: Most database systems provide tools to analyze the execution plan of a query. By examining the plan, you can identify bottlenecks and areas for improvement.

- Update statistics. Ensure that your database system has up-to-date statistics on the distribution of data in your tables. This information helps the query optimizer make better decisions when choosing an execution plan.

- Test and monitor: Regularly test your queries and monitor their performance to identify any issues and make adjustments as needed. You can use database profiling and monitoring tools to gather performance data and analyze it.

By following these best practices and regularly analyzing your queries, you can significantly improve their performance and ensure that your database system operates efficiently. Remember that performance tuning is an ongoing process, as database usage patterns and data can change over time.

Summary

We started by discussing transactions and the ACID properties (Atomicity, Consistency, Isolation, Durability), which ensure database reliability and maintain data integrity during concurrent access. We then demonstrated transactions in practice, using a sample SQL database and executing operations with COMMIT and ROLLBACK to manage transaction states.

Next, we explored stored procedures and functions, which are reusable pieces of SQL code that can be called from applications or other SQL statements. We highlighted the differences between the two and demonstrated how to create and use stored procedures and functions in the context of our sample database. Triggers were the following topic; these are automatic actions that the database executes in response to specified events (e.g., INSERT, UPDATE, DELETE). We provided an in-depth explanation of triggers, created sample triggers on our test database, and discussed their practical applications. Index optimization came next, emphasizing the importance of indexes in improving database performance. We explored techniques for creating and maintaining efficient indexes, such as choosing the right type of index, selecting the appropriate columns, and updating statistics.

Finally, we focused on query performance tuning, a crucial aspect of maintaining a high-performing database system. We provided an overview of various techniques to optimize SQL queries, including using indexes, limiting result sets, optimizing JOINs, using aggregate functions with GROUP BY, optimizing function usage, analyzing query execution plans, updating statistics, and testing and monitoring queries.

Throughout this chapter, we applied the concepts to a sample database, providing hands-on examples and practical tips for understanding and implementing advanced SQL features. The knowledge acquired in this chapter will enable you to work with complex database systems, optimize their performance, and ensure data integrity and reliability.

CHAPTER 11: SAMPLE PROGRAMS & EXECUTING SQL

Sample Program #1

To summarize the learnings from all 10 chapters, let us create a sample database and practice each concept step by step.

Create New Database

First, create a new database named "SampleDB."

```
CREATE DATABASE SampleDB;
```

Create Tables

Create tables for the sample database, following best practices from Chapter 5.

```
CREATE TABLE Users (
  id INTEGER PRIMARY KEY,
  first_name TEXT NOT NULL,
  last_name TEXT NOT NULL,
  email TEXT UNIQUE NOT NULL,
  age INTEGER
);
```

```
CREATE TABLE Orders (
  id INTEGER PRIMARY KEY,
  user_id INTEGER,
  product_name TEXT NOT NULL,
  quantity INTEGER NOT NULL,
  order_date DATE NOT NULL,
  FOREIGN KEY (user_id) REFERENCES Users (id)
);
```

Insert Data

Insert sample data into the tables using the techniques learned in Chapter 3.

```
INSERT INTO Users (first_name, last_name, email, age)
```

```sql
VALUES ('John', 'Doe', 'john.doe@email.com', 30),
    ('Jane', 'Smith', 'jane.smith@email.com', 28);
```

```sql
INSERT INTO Orders (user_id, product_name, quantity, order_date)
VALUES (1, 'Laptop', 1, '2022-01-01'),
    (2, 'Smartphone', 2, '2022-01-03'),
    (1, 'Tablet', 3, '2022-01-05');
```

Query Data

Perform queries on the sample data using techniques from Chapters 3 and 4.

```sql
-- Select all users
SELECT * FROM Users;
```

```sql
-- Select all orders, ordered by order_date
SELECT * FROM Orders
ORDER BY order_date;
```

```sql
-- Count orders per user
SELECT user_id, COUNT(*) as order_count
FROM Orders
GROUP BY user_id;
```

Working with Multiple Tables

Perform JOIN operations using concepts from Chapter 6.

```sql
-- Retrieve user information along with their orders
SELECT Users.*, Orders.*
FROM Users
JOIN Orders ON Users.id = Orders.user_id;
```

Using SQL Functions

Apply SQL functions from Chapter 7 to manipulate data.

```sql
-- Calculate the average age of users
SELECT AVG(age) as average_age
FROM Users;
```

Subqueries and Derived Tables

Practice subqueries and derived tables from Chapter 8.

```sql
-- Find users who have placed more than one order
SELECT *
FROM Users
WHERE id IN (
  SELECT user_id
  FROM Orders
  GROUP BY user_id
  HAVING COUNT(*) > 1
);
```

Views and Materialized Views

Create and use views from Chapter 9.

```sql
-- Create a view that shows user information along with their orders
CREATE VIEW UserOrders AS
SELECT Users.*, Orders.*
FROM Users
JOIN Orders ON Users.id = Orders.user_id;

-- Query the view
SELECT * FROM UserOrders;
```

<u>Advanced SQL</u>

Apply techniques from Chapter 10, such as transactions and performance tuning.

```sql
-- Begin a transaction
BEGIN;


-- Update user age and order quantity
UPDATE Users SET age = 31 WHERE id = 1;
UPDATE Orders SET quantity = 4 WHERE id = 3;


-- Commit the transaction
COMMIT;
```

This sample program covers various aspects of SQL from all 10 chapters, including creating and managing tables, querying data, working with multiple tables, using SQL functions, subqueries, derived tables, views, materialized views, and advanced SQL concepts such as triggers and stored procedures. By practicing these concepts in the context of a sample database, you can reinforce your understanding of the various topics covered throughout the chapters and gain valuable hands-on experience with SQL.

Sample Program #2

Let us create another sample database called "LibraryDB" to manage a library system. We'll create tables for books, authors, and borrowers, and practice SQL concepts from various chapters.

<u>Create New Database</u>

First, create a new database named "LibraryDB."

```sql
CREATE DATABASE LibraryDB;
```

<u>Create Tables</u>

Create tables for the library database following best practices from Chapter 5.

```sql
CREATE TABLE Authors (
```

```sql
  id INTEGER PRIMARY KEY,
  first_name TEXT NOT NULL,
  last_name TEXT NOT NULL
);
```

```sql
CREATE TABLE Books (
  id INTEGER PRIMARY KEY,
  title TEXT NOT NULL,
  author_id INTEGER NOT NULL,
  publication_year INTEGER,
  available BOOLEAN NOT NULL DEFAULT 1,
  FOREIGN KEY (author_id) REFERENCES Authors (id)
);
```

```sql
CREATE TABLE Borrowers (
  id INTEGER PRIMARY KEY,
  name TEXT NOT NULL,
  email TEXT UNIQUE NOT NULL
);
```

```sql
CREATE TABLE BorrowedBooks (
  id INTEGER PRIMARY KEY,
  book_id INTEGER NOT NULL,
  borrower_id INTEGER NOT NULL,
  borrow_date DATE NOT NULL,
  return_date DATE,
  FOREIGN KEY (book_id) REFERENCES Books (id),
  FOREIGN KEY (borrower_id) REFERENCES Borrowers (id)
);
```

Insert Data

Insert sample data into the tables using the techniques learned in Chapter 3.

```sql
INSERT INTO Authors (first_name, last_name)
VALUES ('George', 'Orwell'),
    ('Aldous', 'Huxley'),
    ('Ray', 'Bradbury');
```

```sql
INSERT INTO Books (title, author_id, publication_year)
VALUES ('1984', 1, 1949),
    ('Animal Farm', 1, 1945),
    ('Brave New World', 2, 1932),
    ('Fahrenheit 451', 3, 1953);
```

```sql
INSERT INTO Borrowers (name, email)
VALUES ('John Doe', 'john.doe@email.com'),
    ('Jane Smith', 'jane.smith@email.com');
```

```sql
INSERT INTO BorrowedBooks (book_id, borrower_id, borrow_date)
VALUES (1, 1, '2023-01-01'),
    (3, 2, '2023-01-02');
```

Query Data

Perform queries on the sample data using techniques from Chapters 3 and 4.

```sql
-- Select all books with their authors
SELECT Books.*, Authors.first_name, Authors.last_name
FROM Books
JOIN Authors ON Books.author_id = Authors.id;
```

```sql
-- Find books that are currently borrowed
SELECT Books.*, Borrowers.name, BorrowedBooks.borrow_date
FROM Books
JOIN BorrowedBooks ON Books.id = BorrowedBooks.book_id
JOIN Borrowers ON BorrowedBooks.borrower_id = Borrowers.id
```

```sql
WHERE BorrowedBooks.return_date IS NULL;
```

Working with Multiple Tables

Perform JOIN operations using concepts from Chapter 6.

```sql
-- Retrieve borrowers along with the books they borrowed
SELECT Borrowers.*, Books.title
FROM Borrowers
JOIN BorrowedBooks ON Borrowers.id = BorrowedBooks.borrower_id
JOIN Books ON BorrowedBooks.book_id = Books.id;
```

Using SQL Functions

Apply SQL functions from Chapter 7 to manipulate data.

```sql
-- Count books per author
SELECT author_id, COUNT(*) as book_count
FROM Books
GROUP BY author_id;
```

Subqueries and Derived Tables

Practice subqueries and derived tables from Chapter 8.

```sql
-- Find authors who have more than one book
SELECT *
FROM Authors
WHERE id IN (
  SELECT author_id
  FROM Books
  GROUP BY author_id
  HAVING COUNT(*) > 1
);
```

```sql
-- Find the total number of books borrowed by each borrower using a derived table
SELECT Borrowers., borrowed_books_count.count
FROM Borrowers
JOIN (
SELECT borrower_id, COUNT() as count
FROM BorrowedBooks
GROUP BY borrower_id
) as borrowed_books_count ON Borrowers.id =
borrowed_books_count.borrower_id;
```

Views and Materialized Views

Create a view from Chapter 9 to simplify querying the data.

```sql
-- Create a view for books with author information
CREATE VIEW BooksWithAuthors AS
SELECT Books.*, Authors.first_name, Authors.last_name
FROM Books
JOIN Authors ON Books.author_id = Authors.id;
```

```sql
-- Use the view to find books published before 1950
SELECT * FROM BooksWithAuthors WHERE publication_year < 1950;
```

Advanced SQL

Practice advanced SQL concepts from Chapter 10.

```sql
-- Create a trigger to update the availability of a book when it is borrowed
CREATE TRIGGER update_book_availability
AFTER INSERT ON BorrowedBooks
BEGIN
  UPDATE Books SET available = 0 WHERE id = NEW.book_id;
END;
```

```sql
-- Create a stored procedure to borrow a book
CREATE PROCEDURE BorrowBook (IN book_id INTEGER, IN borrower_id
INTEGER)
BEGIN
  INSERT INTO BorrowedBooks (book_id, borrower_id, borrow_date)
  VALUES (book_id, borrower_id, date('now'));
  CALL update_book_availability();
END;
```

Just to summarize, it begins with

- Creation of a table called BorrowedBooks to store information about borrowed books.
- Inserts sample data into the BorrowedBooks table.
- Executes advanced queries that include the use of DISTINCT and aggregate functions.
- Demonstrates the use of GROUP BY with HAVING clause.
- Creates a derived table to find the total number of books borrowed by each borrower.
- Constructs a view to simplify querying books with author information and uses the view to find books published before 1950.
- Introduces the concept of triggers by creating a trigger to update the availability of a book when it is borrowed.
- Develops a stored procedure to borrow a book, which utilizes the previously created trigger.

Summary

The two sample programs provided a comprehensive practice opportunity, allowing you to apply a wide range of SQL concepts learned throughout the ten chapters. They covered essential aspects of SQL, including creating tables, inserting data, querying data using various techniques, and manipulating data with functions, subqueries, and derived tables.

In these programs, you worked with a sample database involving books, authors, and borrowers. You practiced filtering, sorting, and aggregating data, as well as implementing different types of joins and unions. Additionally, you used SQL functions such as string, numeric, and date/time functions, and applied GROUP BY and HAVING clauses. Furthermore, you explored advanced concepts like creating views and working with triggers and stored procedures. The programs demonstrated the usefulness of views in simplifying complex queries and the power of triggers and stored procedures in automating and managing database operations.

Overall, the learnings from these two sample programs reinforced your understanding of SQL concepts and their practical applications. They allowed you to experience the process of developing and working with a database, while showcasing the versatility and power of SQL in handling real-world data scenarios.

Index

Epilogue

Many kudos for finishing the "SQL 101 Crash Course"! You should be at the point where you have a basic understanding of SQL foundations, best practices, and advanced approaches by this point. You are now able to execute complicated queries, make use of SQL functions and subqueries, and implement sophisticated SQL techniques in order to achieve optimal performance. You have also learned how to create, alter, and optimize tables.

To help you better retain the information presented here, we've sprinkled the text with a variety of real-world examples and scenarios. When you are faced with real-world database difficulties in your professional life, the hands-on knowledge that you've obtained via working with sample databases will prove to be extremely helpful.

It is important to keep in mind that learning is an ongoing process as you begin your journey toward becoming an expert SQL developer. Because the state of technology changes so quickly, it is critical to continually improve one's knowledge and skill set. You may stay abreast of the most recent advancements in the field of SQL and databases by utilizing one of the numerous available tools, which include online classes, discussion groups, and blogs, for example.

Even though you now have a solid foundation in SQL thanks to this book, there is still a great deal more for you to investigate and learn. You might be interested in expanding your knowledge in particular areas of interest, such as database administration, data warehousing, or business intelligence, for example. As your level of expertise increases, you should consider expanding your knowledge of SQL by becoming familiar with additional SQL platforms and tools, such as MySQL, PostgreSQL, or SQL Server. It is essential to develop excellent problem-solving skills and the capacity to think analytically if you want to have a career as a SQL developer. You will not only be able to advance more quickly in your profession if you have these talents, but you will also be better equipped to adjust to any new technology or problems that come your way.

We have high hopes that the "SQL 101 Crash Course" has equipped you with the information, skills, and self-assurance necessary to succeed as a SQL developer. Keep in mind that the only way to truly master something is through repeated practice, so keep probing, experimenting, and improving your SQL skills. We are grateful that you have decided to purchase this book, and we wish you success in all of your future activities as an intelligent SQL developer. I hope that each step of your journey brings you new and interesting challenges, opportunities to expand your knowledge, and professional development.

Thank You

Made in the USA
Monee, IL
07 July 2026